CW01197182

PICTURING TIME

With best Compliments

CREDIT SUISSE

50 YEARS OF
EXCEPTIONAL IMAGES
AND THE STORIES
BEHIND THEM
~

{86}

PICTURING TIME

THE GREATEST PHOTOGRAPHS OF

RAGHU RAI

ALEPH

ALEPH BOOK COMPANY
An independent publishing firm
promoted by **Rupa Publications India**

First published in India in 2015 by
Aleph Book Company
7/16 Ansari Road, Daryaganj
New Delhi 110002

Copyright © Raghu Rai 2015

All rights reserved.

No part of this publication may be reproduced, transmitted, or stored in a retrieval system, in any form or by any means, without permission in writing from Aleph Book Company.

ISBN: 978-93-84067-18-2

3 5 7 9 10 8 6 4 2

Digital Work: Amit Chauhan

Book design: Bena Sareen

Printed and bound in India by
Thomson Press India Ltd., Faridabad

This book is sold subject to the condition that it shall not, by way of trade or otherwise, be lent, resold, hired out, or otherwise circulated without the publisher's prior consent in any form of binding or cover other than that in which it is published.

Title page} Dust storm in Rajasthan, 1969

There was a drought in Rajasthan that year and the Centre had allocated massive funds for drought relief. One of the programmes being funded was the building of roads to generate employment but sadly the government of Mohan Lal Sukhadia, the Rajasthan chief minister, was not up to the task. The prime minister had arrived to inspect the project. However, she had barely begun her inspection tour when she received a telegram informing her that President Zakir Hussain had had a heart attack and passed away. A helicopter arrived to whisk her away and suddenly the metaphoric dust that Sukhadia was throwing into the eyes of his people became real as sand was sprayed everywhere as Mrs Gandhi's aircraft lifted off.

Following page} Dargah in Kerala, circa 1990

End June,
When summer is at its hottest,
When the deep, dense and dusty clouds start to roll in—I am the very
first raindrop of the pre-monsoon sky—
I can't wait any longer...here I go...to merge and seek!

रगों में दौड़ते फिरने के हम नहीं हैं काय़ल
जो आँख ही से न टपका, वो फिर लहू क्या है।

~

ये तस्वीरें मैं समर्पित करता हूँ
उन सभी भारत वासियों को
जिनके दर्शन में, मैंने
ये क्षण पाये।

(I dedicate these images to all those countrymen
who have blessed me with these moments as their Darshan.)

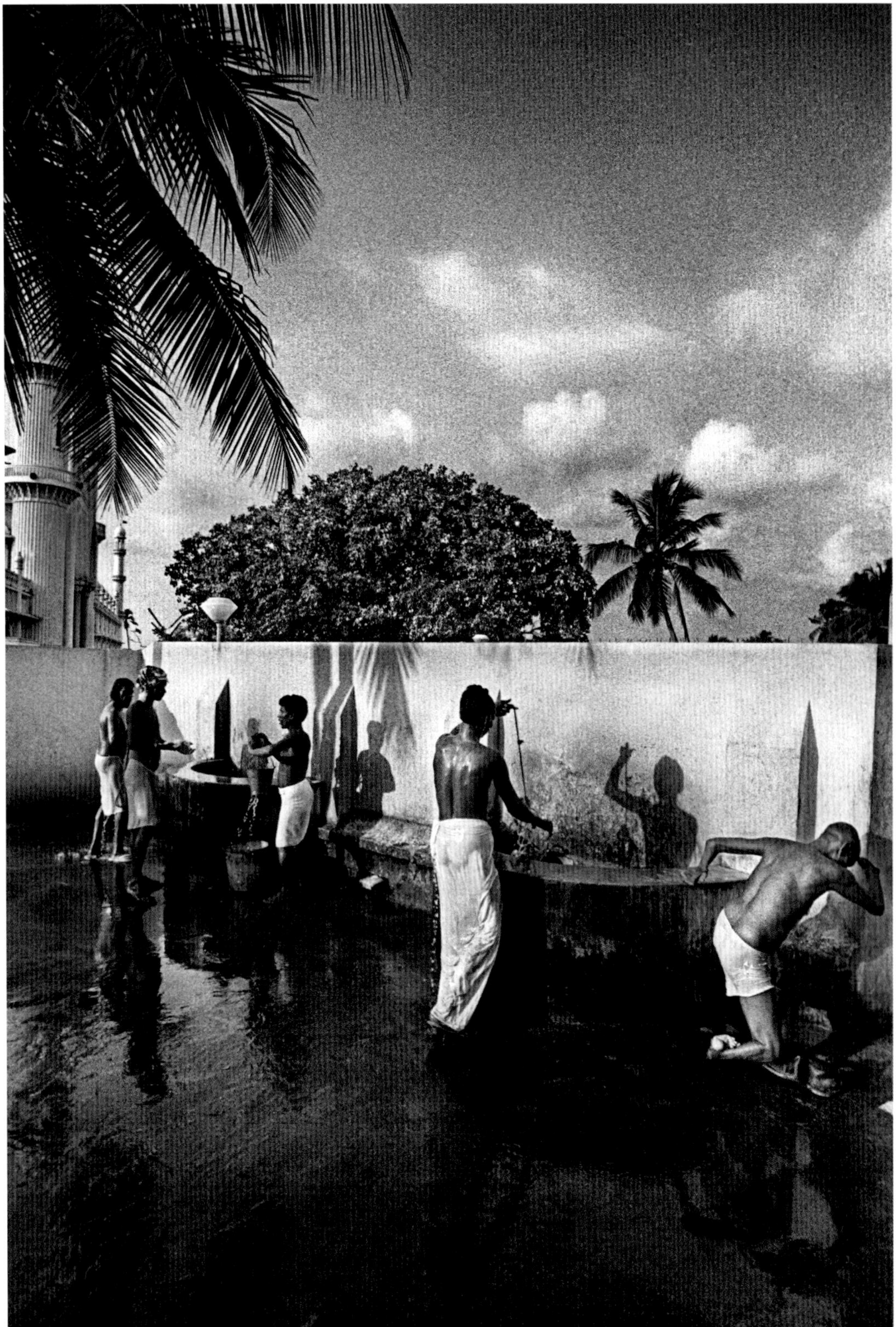

Introduction

In *The Prophet*, Kahlil Gibran writes:

Your children are not your children.
They are the sons and daughters of Life's longing for itself.
They come through you but not from you...

Life's longing for itself—that is what I feel my photographs should reflect. Closer home, we have the divine concept of darshan, which is very precious to me. Darshan is not merely seeing a particular person or place, but the experiencing of the reality of a place, a person, the physical and the inner aura, reflected in its entirety—that is darshan. That is what I feel great photography is all about.

    I began taking pictures in my mid twenties. At the time I was a civil engineer and had a government job for a year but my heart was not in it at all. So I came to live with my elder brother, S. Paul, in Delhi. My brother was chief photographer at the *Indian Express* and Kishore Parekh was chief photographer at the *Hindustan Times*. People noticed their work and began talking about good photographs appearing in these Indian newspapers. Both Paul and Parekh were more than a decade senior than I, and would have an inspiring influence on me. I worked with Kishore Parekh at the *Hindustan Times* for a year and quit the job to join a friend, Rajinder Puri, who was bringing out an evening paper called *Lok*. The experiment ran for three months before funds dried up. I hadn't told my parents that I'd quit my job with *HT* or mentioned anything about the evening paper. I ran away to Corbett Park for a week. My family began looking for me. When I finally told them, they were disappointed. In later years, whenever anyone asked my father, 'How many sons do you have?' He would reply, 'I had four sons, and two have gone photographers.' He could as well have said we had 'gone crazy'.

    In the 1960s, *The Statesman* was a very well-respected newspaper; Ivan Charlton, an Englishman, was its editor. Their brand of journalism was so clear and strong and committed. The chief photographer at the time was retiring, so I applied, and got the job. And so it was that in 1965, Kishore Parekh was the chief photographer at the *Hindustan Times*, my elder brother Paul was chief at the *Indian Express*, and I was in-charge of the photo department at *The Statesman*. I knew Paul and Parekh were brilliant photographers and found myself sandwiched between these two big guys. When you're in a situation like that, you either get crushed or you sprout, and I was lucky to have the initial encouragement from my brother which ensured that I sprouted and started growing in my own way in this field.

~

One of my brother's close friends, Yog Joy, originally a landowner/farmer was becoming a keen photographer. A very warm and gentle human being, he had come to visit Paul and was planning to go back to his village, about 50 km from Delhi, to visit his farm and take pictures. Since I liked him for being what he was, and since I wasn't doing anything at the time, I decided to go with him for two-three days and on a whim asked my brother to give me a camera. He loaded film in an Agfa Super Sillete, a small camera, for me and briefly explained how to operate the exposure and focus. We reached Yog's village that afternoon. While he was photographing the village children in the streets, I stood around watching. Suddenly on the other side, I saw a baby donkey, looking cute and strange. As I went closer to take a picture, the baby donkey started running and the children had a hearty laugh. Then I deliberately began chasing the donkey to amuse the children further. Finally, the baby donkey grew exhausted and came to a standstill, and I took a picture and I got this close-up of its face in soft focus, my first photograph.

When I came back to Delhi, my brother got the film processed and much to my surprise, he picked up this image and said that it was a very good photograph. To which I said, 'O yeah?'

This was the picture my brother sent to *The Times* in London. In the mid 1960s *The Times* used to print a half-page photo every weekend of something unusual, funny, strange or ironic. The picture editor there was Norman Hall, who went on to be editor of the British Journal of Photography annual and had previously edited the reputed *Photography* magazine in the UK where he famously published portfolios of master photographers of that time like Henri Cartier-Bresson, Margaret Bourke-White and Bill Brandt. He published it as a half-page picture in the paper with my byline and that was the beginning of my journey as a photographer.

~

In 1982, I was doing my second book on Delhi and walking around Old Delhi. It's a place that has always been important to me because of its character, its architecture, the heritage and life in the streets and by-lanes—it's another world altogether. I had been taking pictures around Jama Masjid when Saeed Bhai, a local MLA, a tall, nice gentleman approached me and asked what I was doing. He had noticed me earlier and was curious to know why I was wandering around the area with a camera. When I explained that I was doing a picture book on Delhi, and that Jama Masjid and Old Delhi were both special places to me, he asked me to follow him and promised that I would not be disappointed by what I saw.

So we walked to his place through a maze of lanes and climbed to the roof, the highest point in the area, and suddenly the entire city lay in front of me. On one side was Jama Masjid, to my right was the Red Fort, along with a splendid display of other buildings, all old and Mughal architecture, and on the other side was New Delhi—Connaught Place with its modern buildings and skyscrapers coming up. I think it was late August or early September, when the evenings get pleasant, and there were people everywhere, sitting on rooftops, children playing and flying kites. I took a lot of pictures before the sun went down. It was getting dark and I thought no point clicking now, the light was very low.

Though I had taken a lot of photographs that day something was amiss—I hadn't been able to 'connect with the energies in a specific way' that would capture the strength and spirit of the enormous experience of standing where I was, above the city. Just as I was coming down the stairs—and these were open steps, not covered from the top—I saw this lady praying in a house across from where I stood. I looked up and there were these clouds over Jama Masjid, I took a few quick pictures but I was scared because the light was low and it was slow exposure. Luckily, it wasn't a hundred per cent sharp, but sharp enough. 'Evening Prayer' won me a gold in an international competition and recently got published as a full-page in *The Guardian*.

Later, I took the book to Saeed bhai and also made a big print and had it framed for him. We remained in touch for many years. I recount this story not only because it relates the events behind one of my most iconic pictures but also because it illustrates my belief that when you invest so much and try to connect with every inch of space, then there are moments when Nature blesses you with something. This was such a moment. Imagine if Jama Masjid was not there, or if the clouds weren't there, or any of the elements—this picture is like a blessing.

Kehte hain ke kann kann mein bhagvan hai. They say that God exists in every grain. This is not to say that you lift a stone and you will find God. The ability to connect. With anything and everything. Significant or mundane. Precious or ordinary. When you start caring for everything, everything around you starts caring for you in some way or the other, so you stand connected. You connect with every inch of space and respond. It's having a complete awareness of things, and by that I mean not only the physical but also the emotional and spiritual aspect. Even a breeze blowing—what does it do to you and the entire space around you? This is what is so magical about human life and the human spirit—that some people appear from somewhere, some situations arise from somewhere to bless you with the unexpected—and that is darshan. This is the way I look at it.

If people can connect with my pictures and enjoy them that is enough for me. It's like you are walking down the street and you smile at someone and they smile back. There is nothing given and nothing taken. It is just like a little nudge, a recognition of humanity and life. That is what photography means to me. It is my profession, it is my life, it is my karma, it is my dharma.

~

1960s

I began my career as a professional photographer in 1965 when I started working for the *Hindustan Times*. This decade saw some historic moments in Indian politics; from this decade, until 1990, I spent a vast amount of time capturing these moments. In the early years of my profession, my brother, S. Paul, and Kishore Parekh were an inspiring influence for me. During this time, I witnessed three very significant events—the death of Lal Bahadur Shastri, the split in the Indian National Congress and the birth of my son.

~

Above} Baby donkey, 1965

Right} Sparrows, Chawri Bazaar, circa 1965

The sparrows were pecking at grains when I was standing looking at them through the viewfinder. It was interesting, but not interesting enough. Then suddenly the big black intruder appeared. Instead of scurrying away, they made space for it. I took a picture and the bird flew off; it was as if it had been sent to create a moment for me.

This picture was taken during my early years as a photographer when I was learning to explore; I could constantly feel a sense of wonder and amazement at the gifts photography bestowed on me. Whenever moments like this were offered up, I instinctively grabbed them.

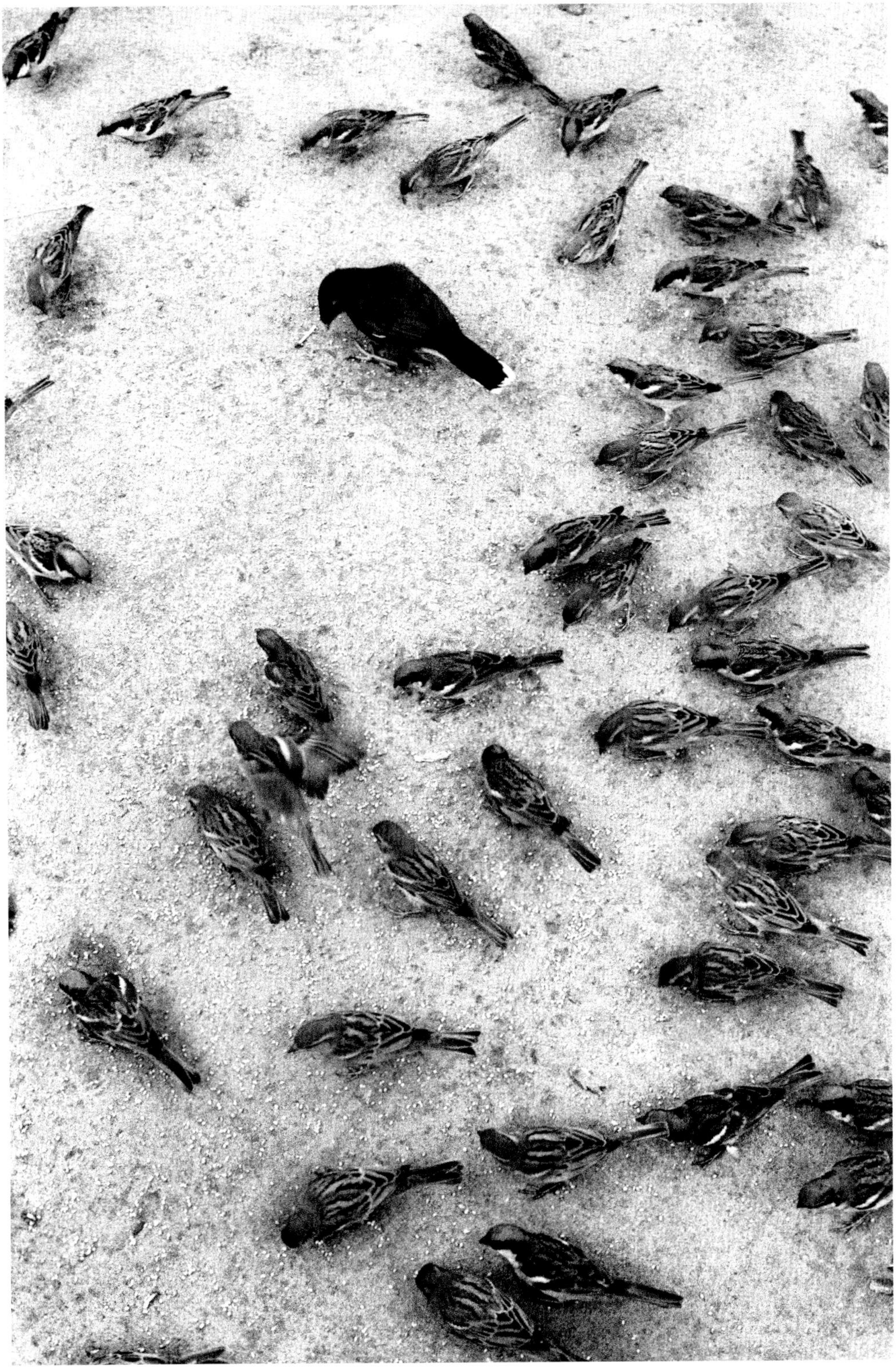

Street scene, Chawri Bazaar, circa 1966

Before I joined the *Hindustan Times* and much before I joined *The Statesman*, I had spent a year on the streets of Delhi taking pictures. This picture of a street scene at Chawri Bazaar in Old Delhi is an image which could have been taken 200 years ago. It epitomizes the multi-layered India of many religions, environments and people and how they have learnt to co-exist side by side at the same time. There is so much going on: rickshaws, trolleys, horse-drawn carriages, bicycles, labourers, schoolchildren; and down the middle the energy of the crisscrossing carriage tracks.

Wheat threshing, Humayun's Tomb, 1966

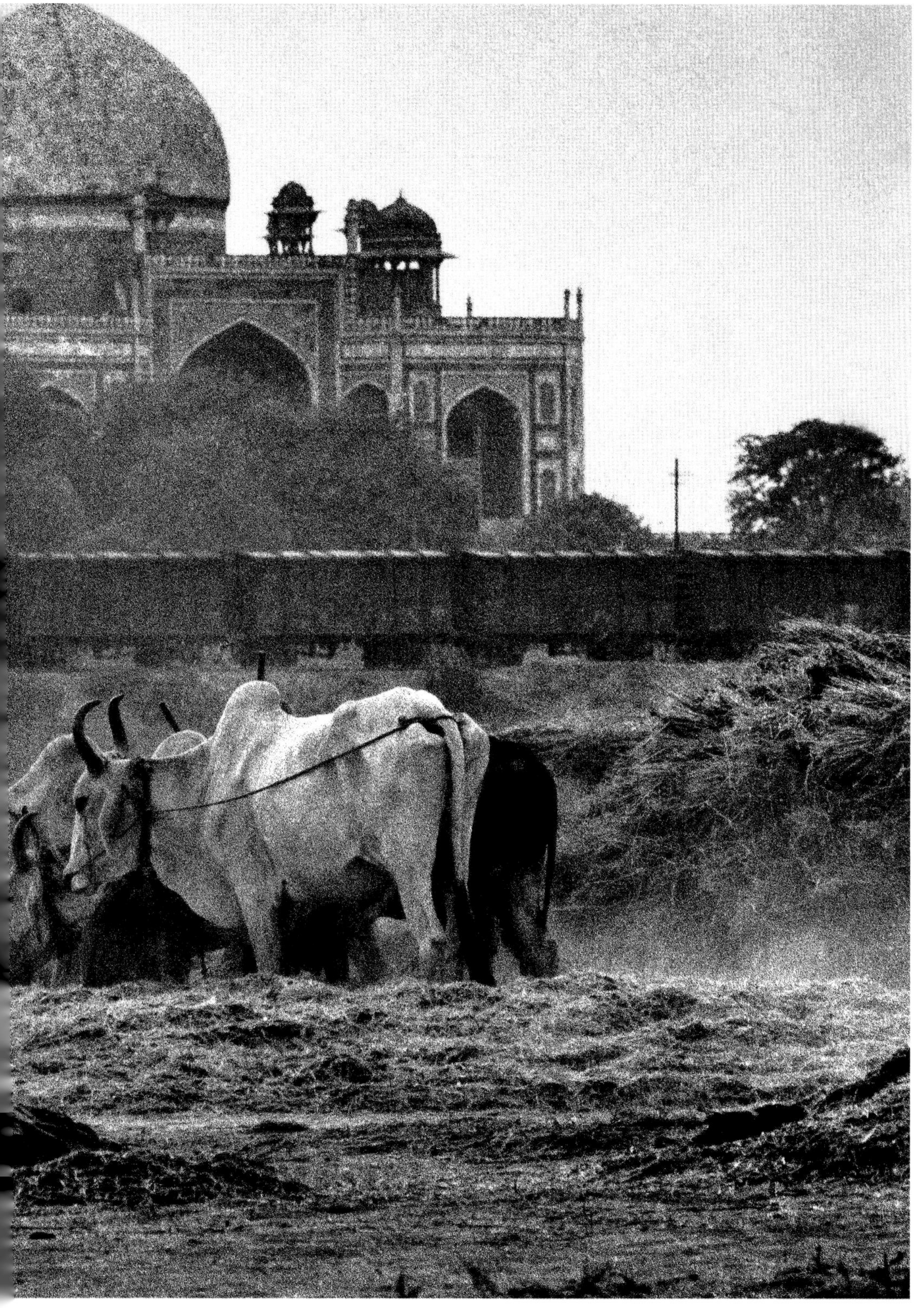

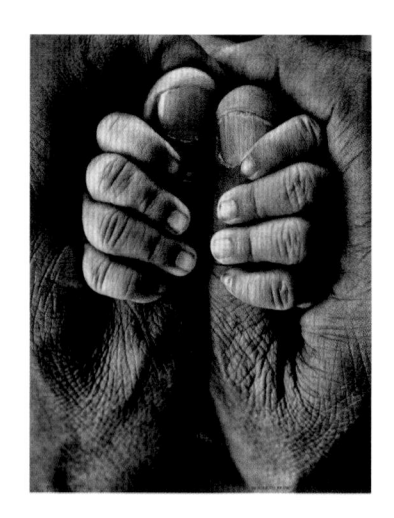

Above} My father and my son, 1969

This is when my first child—my son—was born and my father came to see him. He was holding his little hands and talking to him. I was standing behind him and saw the grandfather's old big hands cushioning the grandchild's tender little ones. This moment called for a picture, so I quickly picked up the camera (I have a camera with me at all times), put my father's hands together and took this picture. So this image has three generations, my father, my son and me.

Right} Boys jump into a village pond, 1969

Way back in 1969, I was a young photographer. On a slow news day, I was photographing these boys jumping into a village pond to beat the heat and humidity of a Delhi summer. It was towards the evening, there were still some clouds overhead but I did not know how to integrate them into the daily lives of these village boys, until suddenly two boys who had climbed up a tall tree, dived towards the pond. I very quickly grabbed my camera with a 28 mm wide lens and captured the moment.

Ever since, the skies were not the limit, in fact, they became a part of my being—a whole new space had opened up for me where life took shelter under the skies.

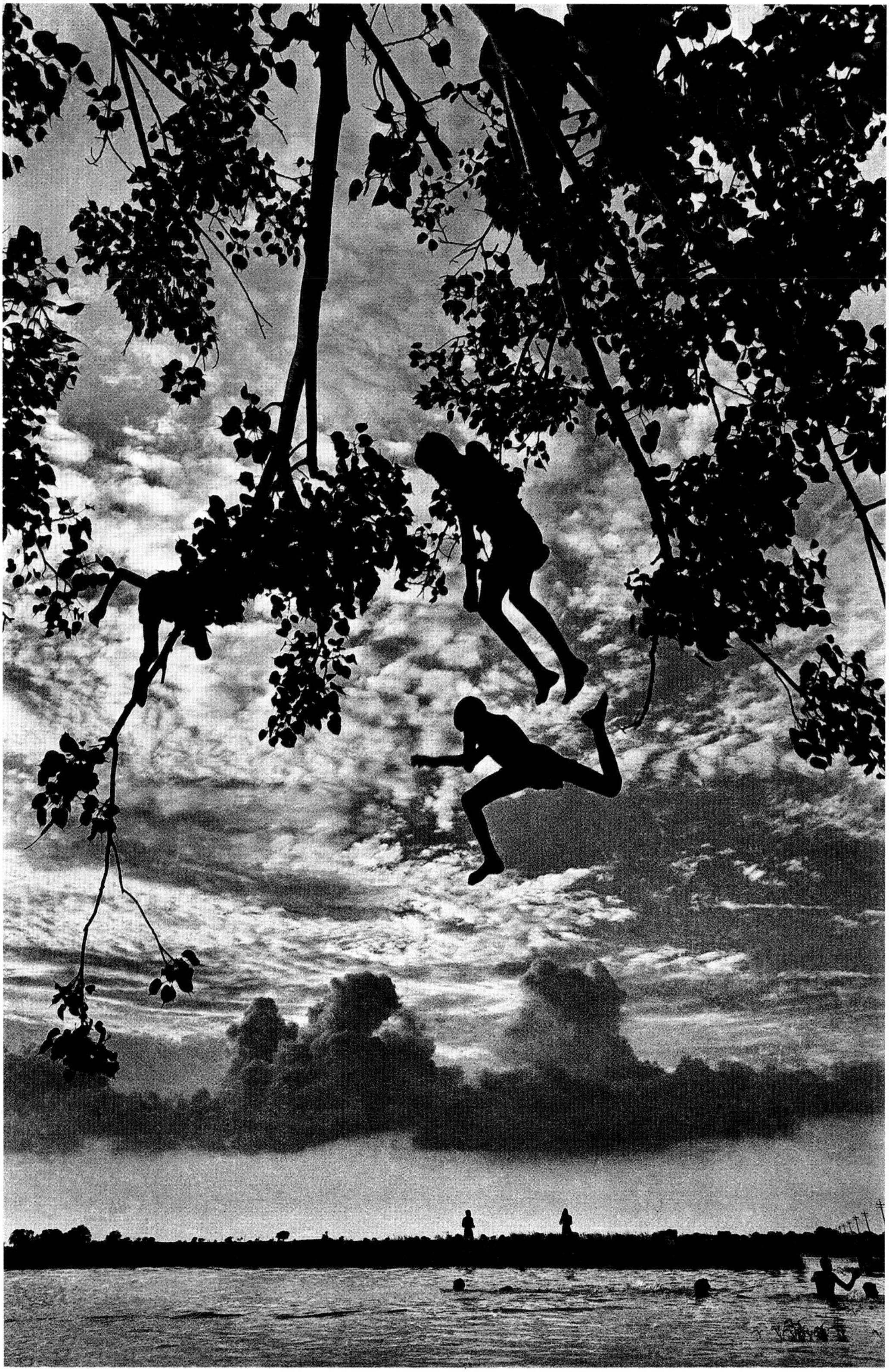

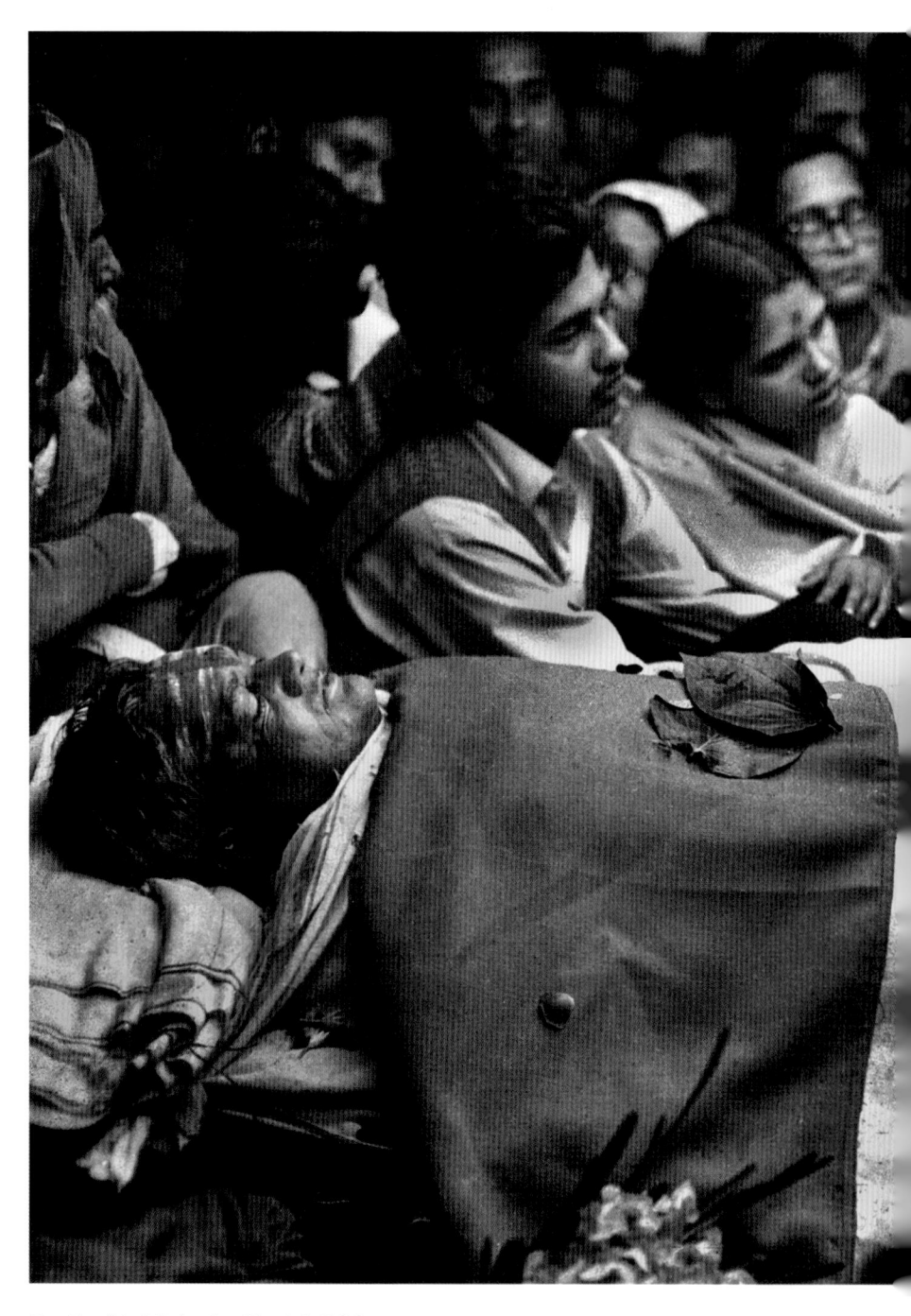

Death of Lal Bahadur Shastri, 1966

I joined *The Statesman* in 1966 as its chief photographer and this was the first major news event I covered. Prime Minister Lal Bahadur Shastri had flown to Tashkent, to sign the Tashkent Declaration with Pakistan's President Ayub Khan.

He died of a sudden heart attack to the shock of the nation. His body was flown back to India. An inconsolable Lalita Shastri can be seen at the extreme right.

Indira Gandhi in a huddle of Congressmen, 1967

The Congressmen are bunched together during the split in the party, planning and conspiring. Even though Mrs Gandhi is standing with them, she's looking beyond, her eyes on the future.

Indira Gandhi in her office late at night, 1968

PICTURING TIME | RAGHU RAI

Indira in a Congress meeting, 1969

It was said of Indira Gandhi that she was 'the only man in her cabinet'. Here she is in a meeting, surrounded by MLAs from Gujarat who had come to her with a proposal. R. K. Dhawan, who was Mrs Gandhi's personal secretary, used to be the guy who handled everything for her. Whatever anybody's agenda, he would help them, he was the middleman between the Congressmen and Mrs Gandhi. And you can see how he, too, is waiting along with all the Congressmen for the Big Boss to sanction papers.

Indira Gandhi at a Congress session, 1966

I was photographing Indira Gandhi almost every other day from 1967 onwards, when she became the prime minister. When I started doing this, I realized that if someone in the future didn't know who she was, and what a strong personality she was, what a tough leader she proved to be, perhaps they would realize that by looking at these photographs. I began to ask myself, does this picture stand the test of time by itself, for itself? These pictures of her capture some of her essence.

1970s

The political landscape of India was transformed in the 1970s. The rise and fall of Indira Gandhi, the Bangladesh War, the Simla Agreement, and the subsequent release of 90,000 prisoners of war by India, there was a lot happening. Our government had been struggling to rehabilitate the refugees pouring in from Bangladesh. Indira Gandhi was at the peak of her career and in a certain way her growth coincided with my career. Then came the Emergency—a twenty-one-month period of utter chaos and commotion in the country. At the time, people were turning to 'Loknayak' Jayaprakash Narayan, a contemporary of Jawaharlal Nehru, and he was rising to fame. It was also in the early 1970s that I first met Mother Teresa.

~

Above} Mother Teresa, 1970

In 1970, I met Mother (Teresa) for the first time. Desmond Doig, one of my editors at *The Statesman*, rang me up one day from Calcutta saying that he had just met a great lady, and that it was imperative that I met and photographed her. These were among the first pictures I took of her, the beginning of a lifelong association that would have a profound influence on me as a human being, as well as a photographer.

Right} This picture of her coming down the stairs, with the crucifix behind her and sunshine touching her feet, captures the spirit of who she was.

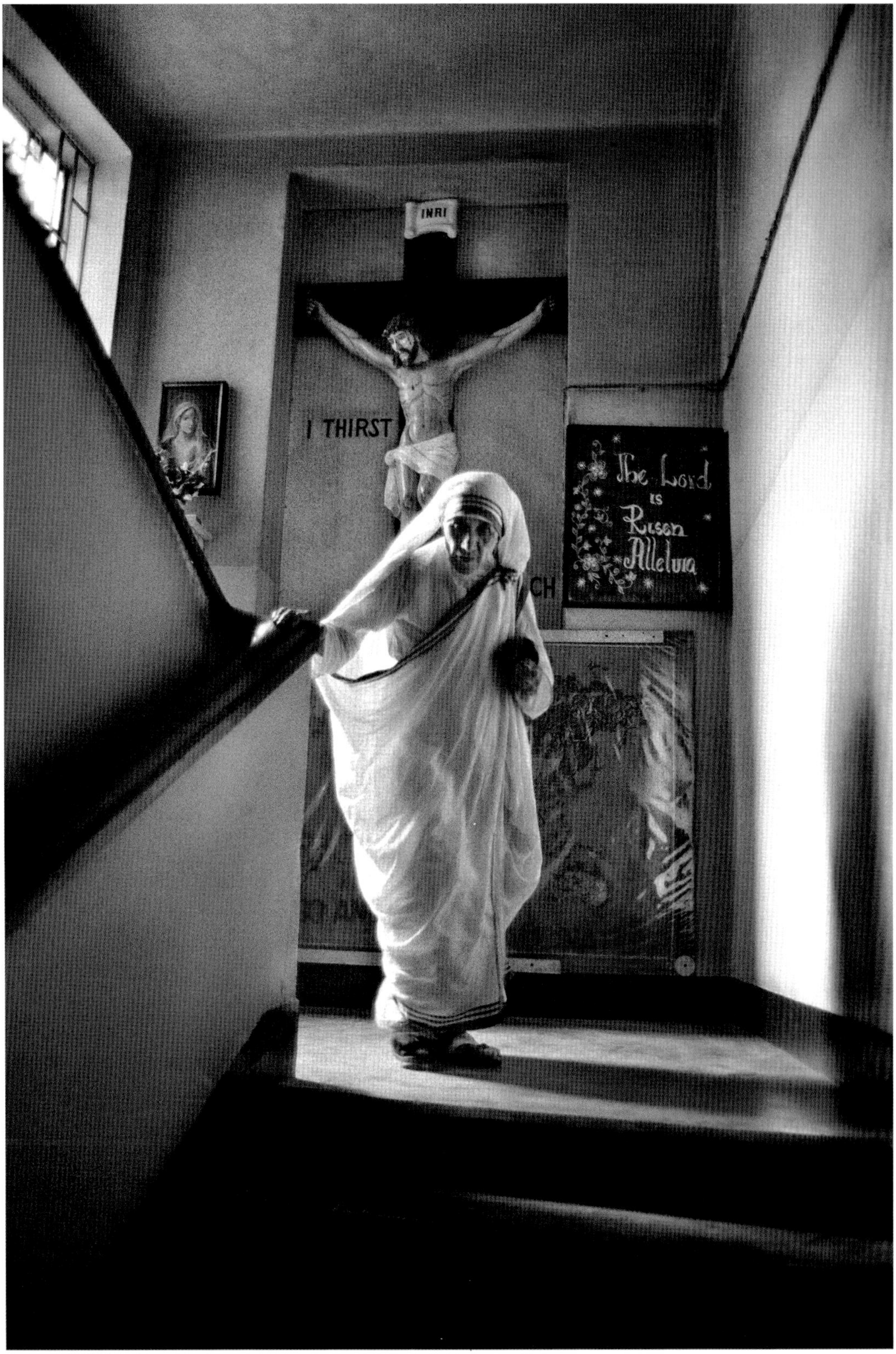
INRI
I THIRST
The Lord is Risen Alleluia
CH

Bangladesh War, 1971

Thousands of refugees were crossing over the border into India. I went to Calcutta when the 1971 war broke out in, what was then, East Pakistan. Thousands of refugees began to pour into India across the border and the government was simply not equipped to deal with a catastrophe of this magnitude. Many of the refugees had to fend for themselves, and lived inside empty sewage pipes, makeshift tents or out in the open. This is in Jessore, which was the first town after the border. There was misery on the faces of the refugees. This woman had her head down and was crying, and crying. Then there were no more tears. She looked up with eyes of stone.

When my three-year-old son saw this photograph he asked me why?

PICTURING TIME | RAGHU RAI

Bangladesh, 1971

This was one of my most important assignments. There was a lot of paranoia at the time and Pakistan's propaganda was very strong. Nobody believed that millions of refugees were coming into the country. When international publications like the *New York Times*, *Sunday Times*, *The Guardian*, *Le Monde* and *Le Figaro* gave these photographs half-page, if not full-page coverage, and TV channels interviewed me, it was the first time the extent of the tragedy became known to the world.

PICTURING TIME | RAGHU RAI

Prisoner of War, 1971 The Indian army with a severely wounded Pakistani soldier who is being taken to Khulna for treatment.

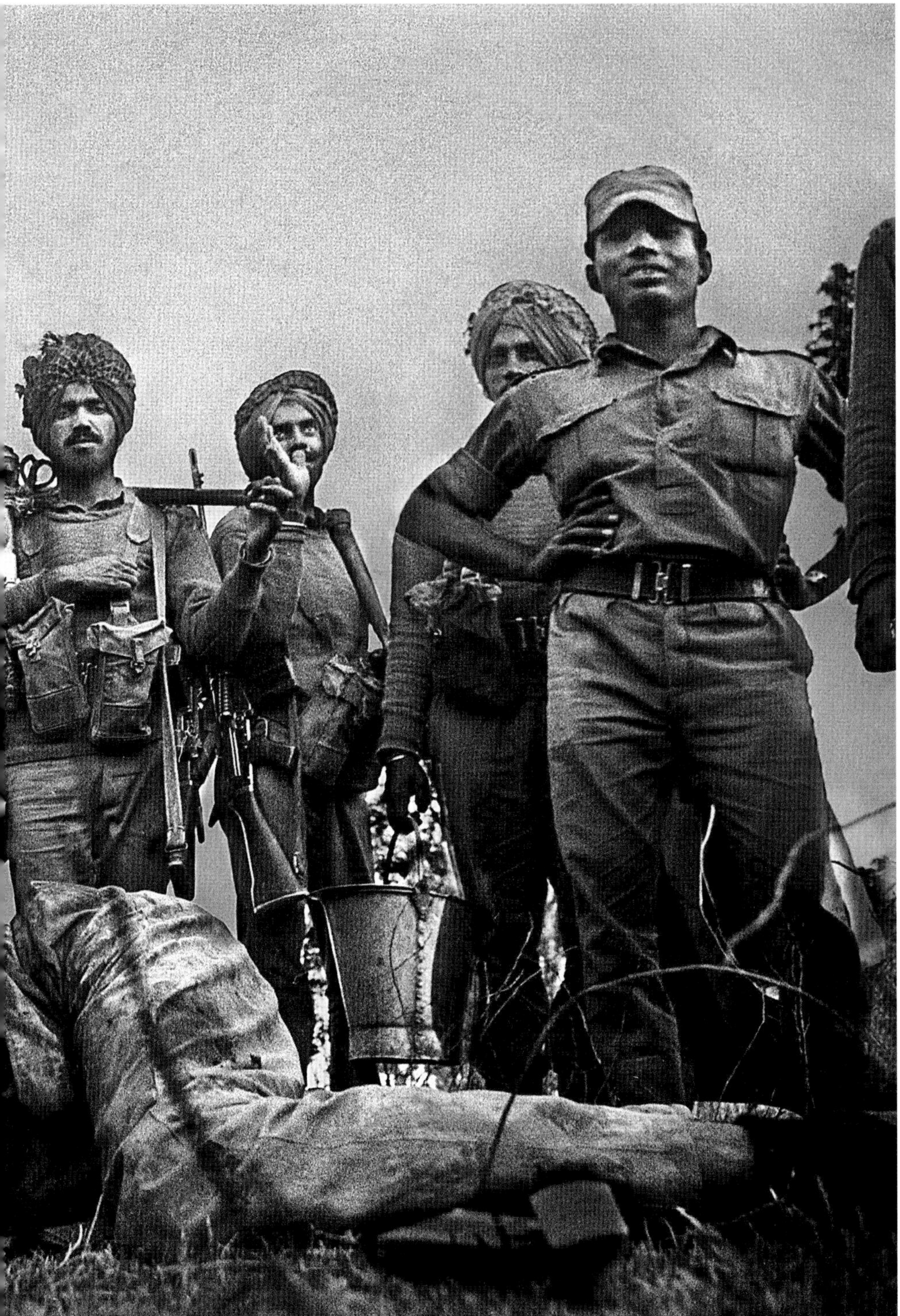

Instrument of Surrender, 16 December 1971

This photo was taken after General A. A. K. Niazi of Pakistan and General Jagjit Singh Aurora signed the Instrument of Surrender, the written agreement that declared the defeat of the Western Pakistani Forces in the Bangladesh Liberation War. The man actually responsible for India winning the war and organizing the surrender was General J. F. R. Jacob. As he was a Jew, when the surrender took place, our government took the strategic decision to exclude him from the ceremony, so it would not seem as though Muslims were surrendering to Jews. That aside, this photograph shows the victorious energy radiating from Indian General Aurora, and the humiliation spilling from the face of Pakistani General Niazi.

General Manekshaw's moustache, 1973

General Sam Manekshaw was the army chief who brilliantly strategized the 1971 war, ensuring that India won. He took quick decisions with the help of Indira Gandhi and Lieutenant General J. F. R. Jacob who briefed him all the way.

In this picture, he is being appointed to the five-star rank of field marshal by President V. V. Giri; the first army chief to receive that title. When he became the chief of army staff there was a captain at the airport who had a longer moustache than him. General Manekshaw said, 'Longer moustache? Not allowed!'

Gandhi and Bhutto in Shimla, 1972

In July 1972, Prime Minister Indira Gandhi and Pakistani President Zulfiqar Ali Bhutto met in Shimla to sign what is now known as the Simla Agreement, which set down the principles for future Indo-Pak relations following the 1971 Liberation War of Bangladesh and resulted in the release of 90,000 prisoners. Bhutto was a very handsome and stylish man. We used to joke back in the day about this picture, and say that it showed 'Mr and Mrs Bhutto'. Somebody put us straight on that account when he said: 'Mr and Mrs Gandhi'.

Indira Gandhi, 1972

Mrs Gandhi loved the Himalayas. While she was in Shimla staying at The Retreat, I requested some time to photograph her. Her secretary, Mr Sharada Prasad, a wonderful man, arranged the session. I was taking pictures of her walking on the lawns, but after a while I stopped and she asked, 'Kya hua?' I said, 'Tasveer achhi nahin ban rahi.' She asked, 'Kya karna hai?' I asked her to climb on to the stone parapet that was blocking my view of the Himalayas. A chair was brought and she stepped on to it. What's interesting about this picture is her hand—it's in a certain mudra.

Smiling Buddha, 1974 In May 1974, India conducted its first nuclear tests at Pokhran. I happened to be in Rajasthan for another story and decided, on a whim, to go there. I had a strange curiosity about Pokhran. We kept driving into the dust and after a few kilometres the road ended and we came upon these patches. The test was over. Everything had been flattened. You can see the cloud, and the trail marks left behind by the hundreds of jeeps that had travelled this path.

Protests, 1975

Jayaprakash Narayan became the rallying point for all those who were opposed to Mrs Gandhi during the turbulent years when she declared a state of Emergency and suspended civil liberties in the country. I was in Patna to meet JP, as he was fondly known. There was a strange tension and silence in the atmosphere, the streets outside were deserted. Although Section 144 had been declared and processions and gatherings of more than four people were forbidden, JP, and the youth from the Yuva Mukti Morcha who had gathered at his house, decided to march in protest. People were waving and cheering from their balconies, and a few hundred yards later, more students came running forward to join the procession. When the crowd swelled and became unmanageable, paramilitary forces were asked to move in, and they stopped JP's procession. He got down from his jeep and started charging ahead with his followers.

Now how would a jawan from Kerala or Punjab know who JP was? The paramilitary began charging him with lathis. Since I was close enough, I took this picture. The next day, *The Statesman* carried it. The question was raised in Parliament—the home minister denied the charge but had to apologize when a copy of the newspaper was thrown at him.

PICTURING TIME | RAGHU RAI

Emergency, 1975

In June 1975, the Allahabad high court declared Indira Gandhi's election to the Lok Sabha void on the grounds of electoral malpractice. Political analysts, politicians and commentators have their own understanding of this complex and chaotic time, but being an instinctive person, I look at it from a more human angle. Mrs Gandhi, being the daughter of Pandit Jawaharlal Nehru, had grown up with a sense of security, and had seen the power her father wielded, the respect he commanded, and she reflected this in her own way.

When the Allahabad HC gave the judgement against her victory, the big question was whether she should resign. At this time, her son, Sanjay Gandhi, who was a strong-willed and headstrong man, was controlling things from behind the scenes. West Bengal Chief Minister Siddhartha Shankar Ray and the chief minister of Haryana, Bansi Lal, both of whom were an integral part of Mrs Gandhi's coterie, caught hold of Sanjay and told him that if Mrs Gandhi resigned, they would lose control; Siddhartha Shankar Ray, being a senior advocate, proposed that a state of Emergency be declared.

It had been a decade since Pandit Nehru's death in 1964, Mrs Gandhi was now insecure and at a loss. When Sanjay rose to the occasion she suddenly found a man in the family she could rely on.

Defeat, 1977

When the elections were held after the Emergency, the mood was overwhelmingly against the Congress. At 5 p.m., when voting was officially over I came across this man near Jama Masjid collecting posters for raddi. On the wall behind him is the infamous 'Hum do, humare do' family planning campaign that turned into a forced sterilization campaign under the aegis of Sanjay Gandhi in the Emergency era. I told my editor, Kuldip Nayar, that this was the only picture I would submit, because it sums up everything and is a stronger image than showing lines of voters or political banners. He saw what I meant and agreed that it was 'very strong' but quickly added that we couldn't publish it, because if Mrs Gandhi won, we would both go to jail. I was adamant about my decision and told him that I knew she would lose, as I had been on the ground and felt the pulse of the people. Besides I've always trusted my intuition deeply. This led to an argument and eventually I tore up the picture and announced that I would not be coming to the office again.

The next day, by five in the evening, the results showed the Janata Party leading substantially. Kuldip Nayar began looking for me and was informed that I had not come to the office. He called me up at my residence and said sorry and the next day this picture was printed prominently on the front page as a photo editorial.

Above} Mrs Gandhi with Acharya Vinoba Bhave, 1977

After her defeat, Mrs Gandhi was at a loss and without an anchor. This photograph shows her at Acharya Vinoba Bhave's ashram near Nagpur seeking personal solace. The Acharya was a freedom fighter and spiritual teacher who began the Bhoodan movement to distribute land to the poor.

Right} JP and Morarji Desai, 1978

Many opposition leaders, journalists and activists who were jailed during the Emergency were released in 1977 when the elections were announced. The opposition parties joined hands under the leadership of JP, rallying under the banner of the Janata Party, which won a massive victory in the elections and became the first non-Congress party to form a government at the Centre. It was JP who supported Morarji Desai to be declared as the next prime minister of the country, although neither he nor his government lasted long.

PICTURING TIME | RAGHU RAI

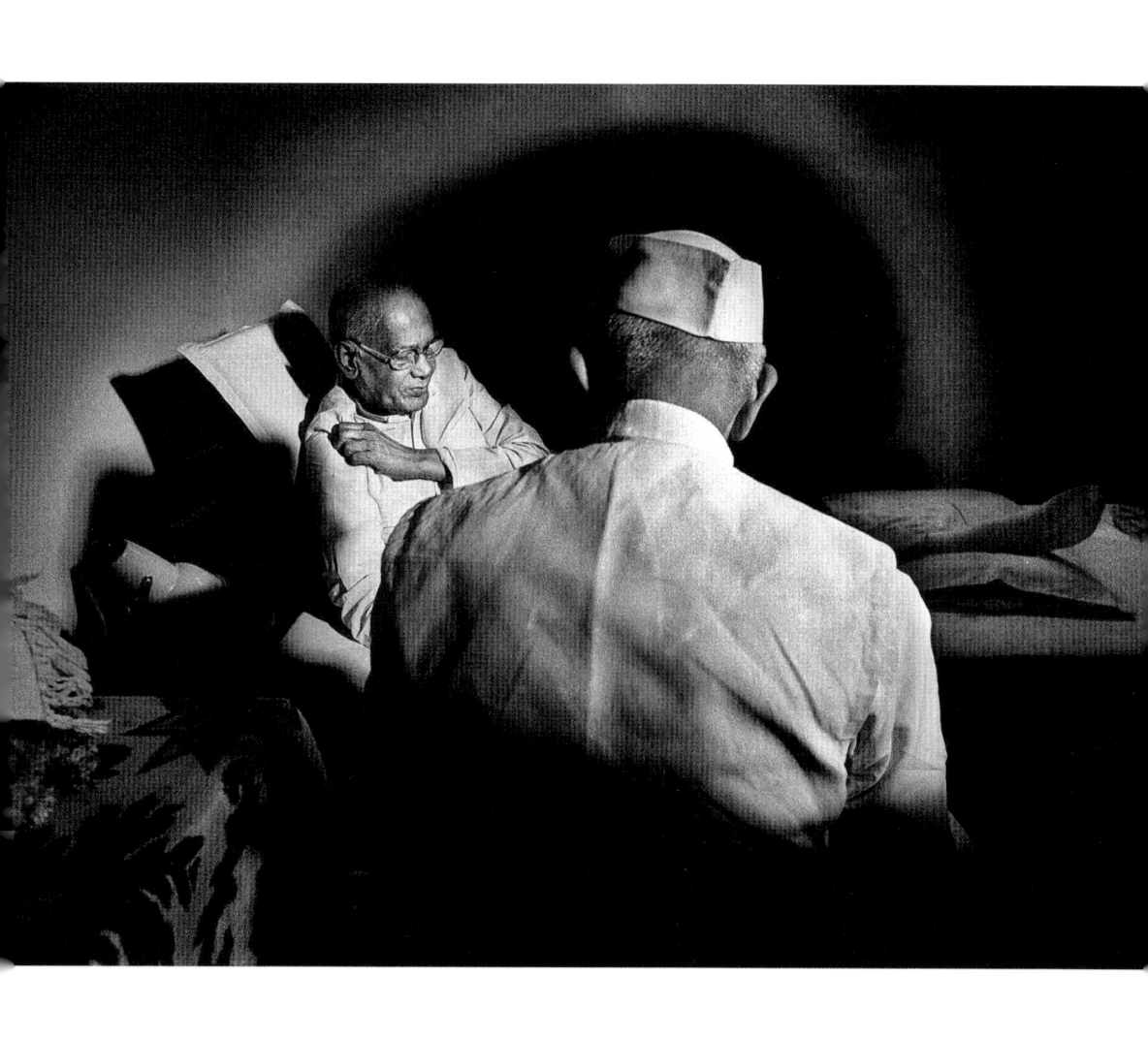

Taj Mahal, 1985

I began photographing the Taj Mahal upon the insistence of Desmond Doig, who felt it needed to be seen from a fresh creative perspective. A few years later, I was flying with Air Force Chief Mulgaonkar over Ladakh where the press was being shown border security exercises carried out by the armed forces. I mentioned to him that I had been taking pictures of the Taj for three to four years and had taken photographs of it from every angle in nearly every season, from the village side, the river side, and there was only one side missing. He smiled and asked me what I wanted. I asked if he could organize a helicopter for me so I could take a picture of the Taj from the air. He immediately called his PR man, Sqn Ldr Malik, to coordinate with Air Force headquarters in Agra, and arranged for me to fly over the Taj Mahal for an hour in the morning and an hour in the evening.

It was an old transport plane and they opened the big hatch with a strong wind blowing through. To keep me from being blown away, two guys held me in a sort of harness. I shot from different angles, it was so profoundly beautiful and fascinating. Even M. F. Husain, himself a painter of such stature, congratulated me on this picture, it was something very special to him.

PICTURING TIME | RAGHU RAI

Kalachakra initiation in Ladakh, 1976

This is the first Kalachakra (Buddhist initiation ceremony) that His Holiness the Dalai Lama initiated in Ladakh, in September 1976. It was raining heavily the whole day and it grew very cold. All the monks were sitting in the rain and their oracle kept blowing the bugle to stop the rain but it continued to pour.

Above} The ghats at Varanasi, 1975

Right} Varanasi, 1975

A woman standing on the ghats after taking a holy dip in the Ganga. An image that was transformed by the bird flying overhead.

Overleaf} Diving at the Baoli, 1971

At the sixteenth-century Agrasen Baoli in Connaught Place when it still had water in it. Years later, the writer Sam Miller showed this picture to the guard at the Baoli and, incredibly, the man said that he was the boy jumping into the water. He had a clipping of my photo as proof.

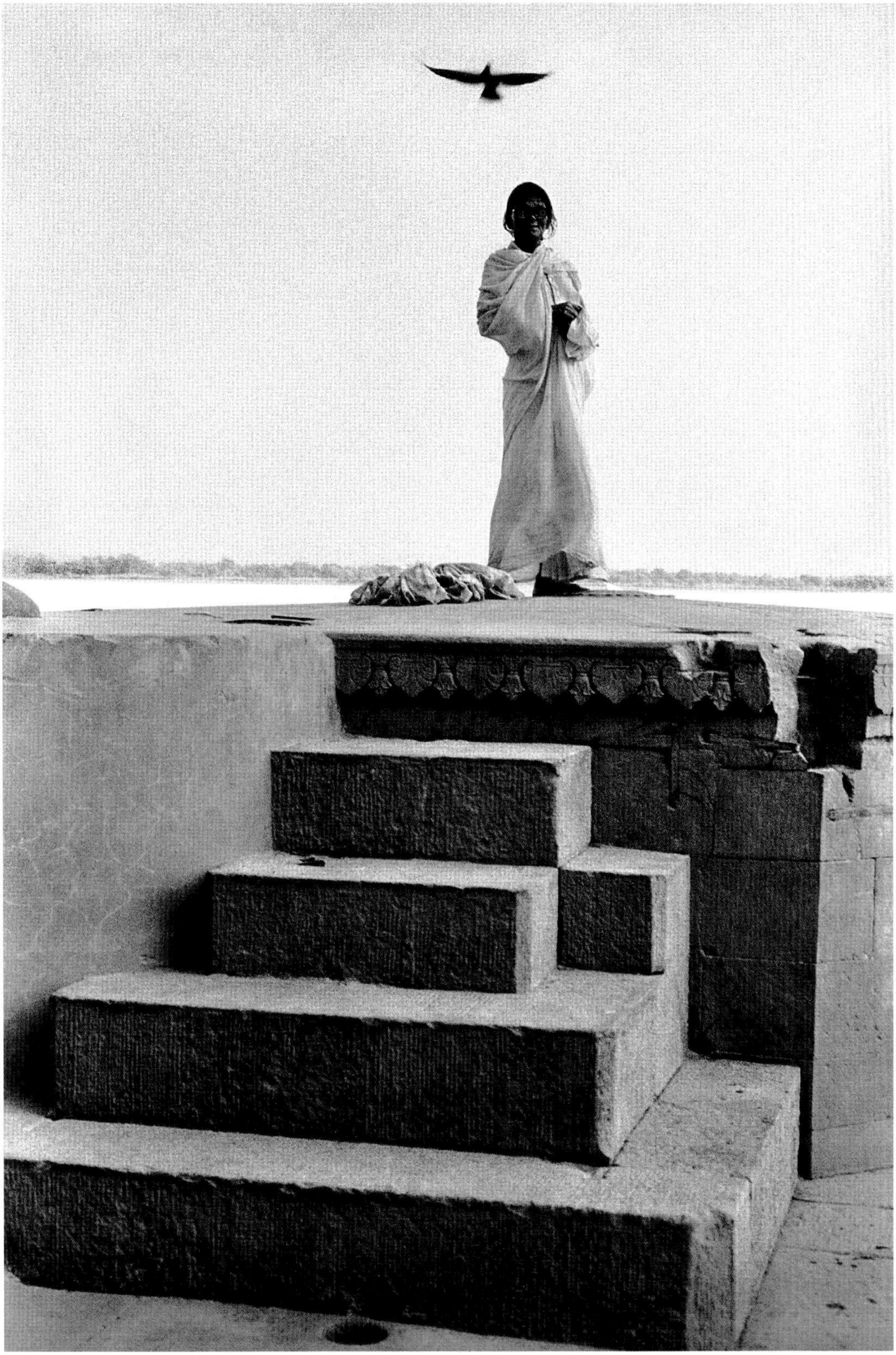

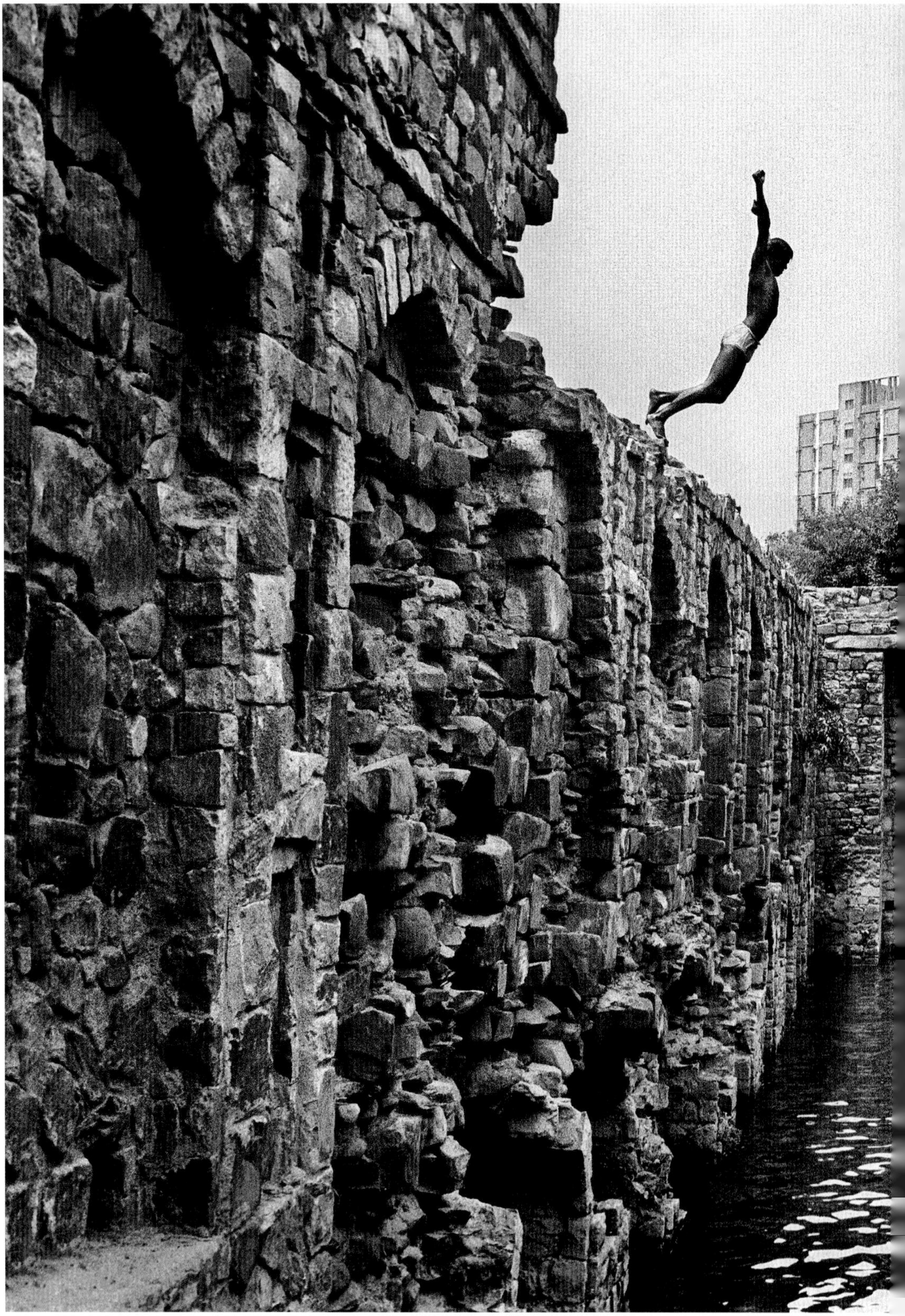

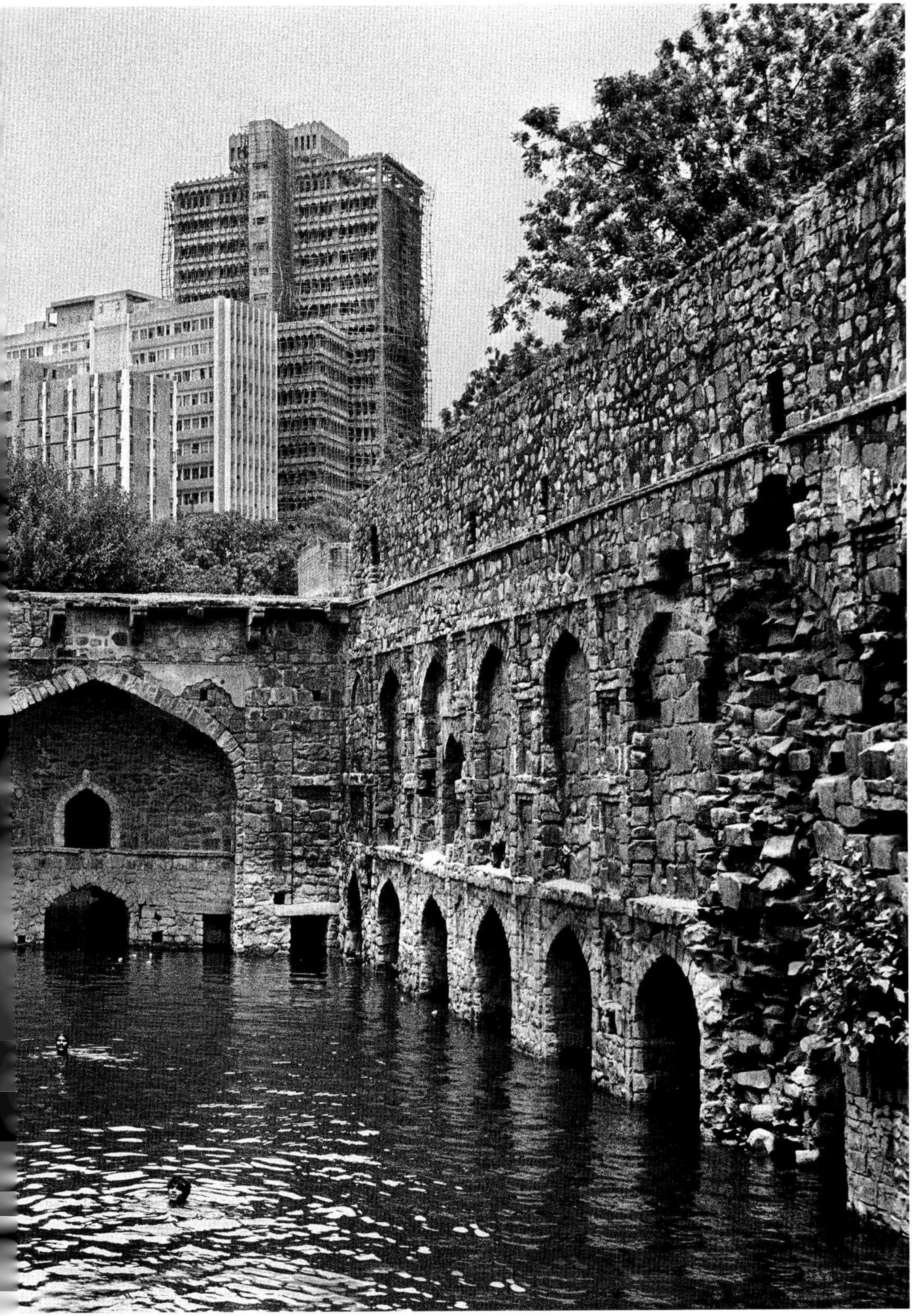

Above} Rocks near Qutab Minar, 1990

Right} Birdie girl, Humayun's Tomb, 1973

PICTURING TIME | RAGHU RAI

The spectrum of life against a wall, circa 1975

During the Emergency, when there were no political rallies or meetings, I would go and sit in front of this wall that connects Darya Ganj to Jama Masjid and photograph life against it. People would scribble their frustrations, art, messages in the form of graffiti.

The streets of Delhi, 1976

I must have followed this cart being pushed by this lady and her husband for half a kilometre, when suddenly the scene expanded into an unforgettable image. When I met Satyajit Ray for the first time, he mentioned this image in particular and told me he could never forget it.

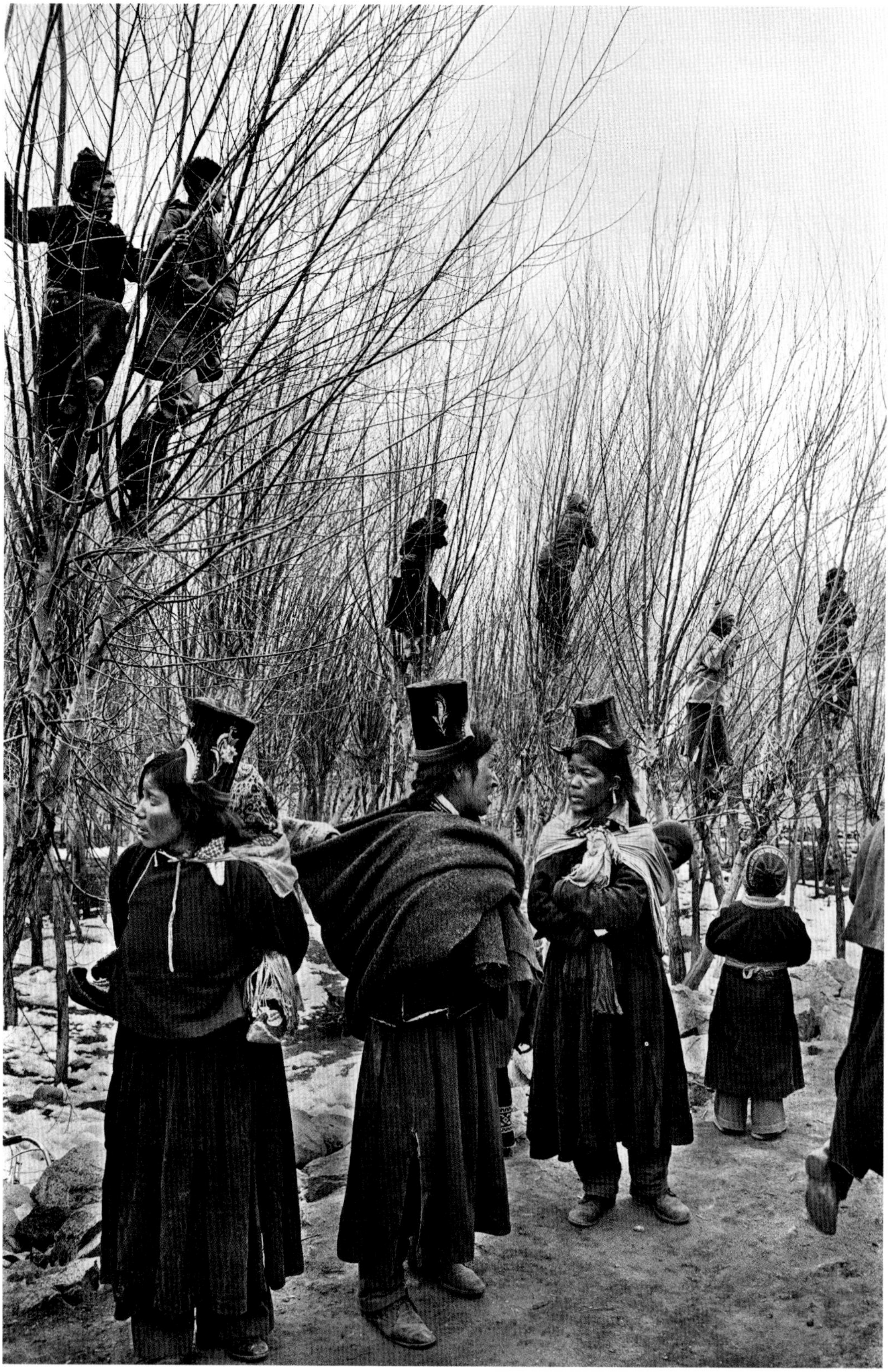

Above} Flash floods in Jaipur, 1977

Left} Ice hockey, 1975

Ladakhi people in a celebratory mood climb trees to watch an ice hockey match. It gives the illusion that they are flying from tree to tree, like in some Shaolin film.

1980s

The montage of India in the 1980s is an odd mishmash of cataclysmic incidents such as the Bhopal Gas Tragedy and the assassination of Mrs Gandhi, and pleasant interactions I had with the gurus of Indian classical music such as Bhimsen Joshi, M. S. Subbulakshmi, Pandit Ravi Shankar, S. Balachander and Ustad Bismillah Khan.

I got my most challenging project in 1984—Operation Blue Star. Post the shootout at the Akal Takht, the army had forbidden people from taking pictures inside the temple complex, and they were checking all the bags. So I bought a whole lot of garlands and buried a small camera—loaded with film and the exposure already set— deep inside a bag full of the garlands.

I managed to sneak my camera into the temple complex. I had two friends, one shielding me from the left, another from the right and in this way I managed to take pictures of the Akal Takht.

~

Evening prayer, Jama Masjid, 1982

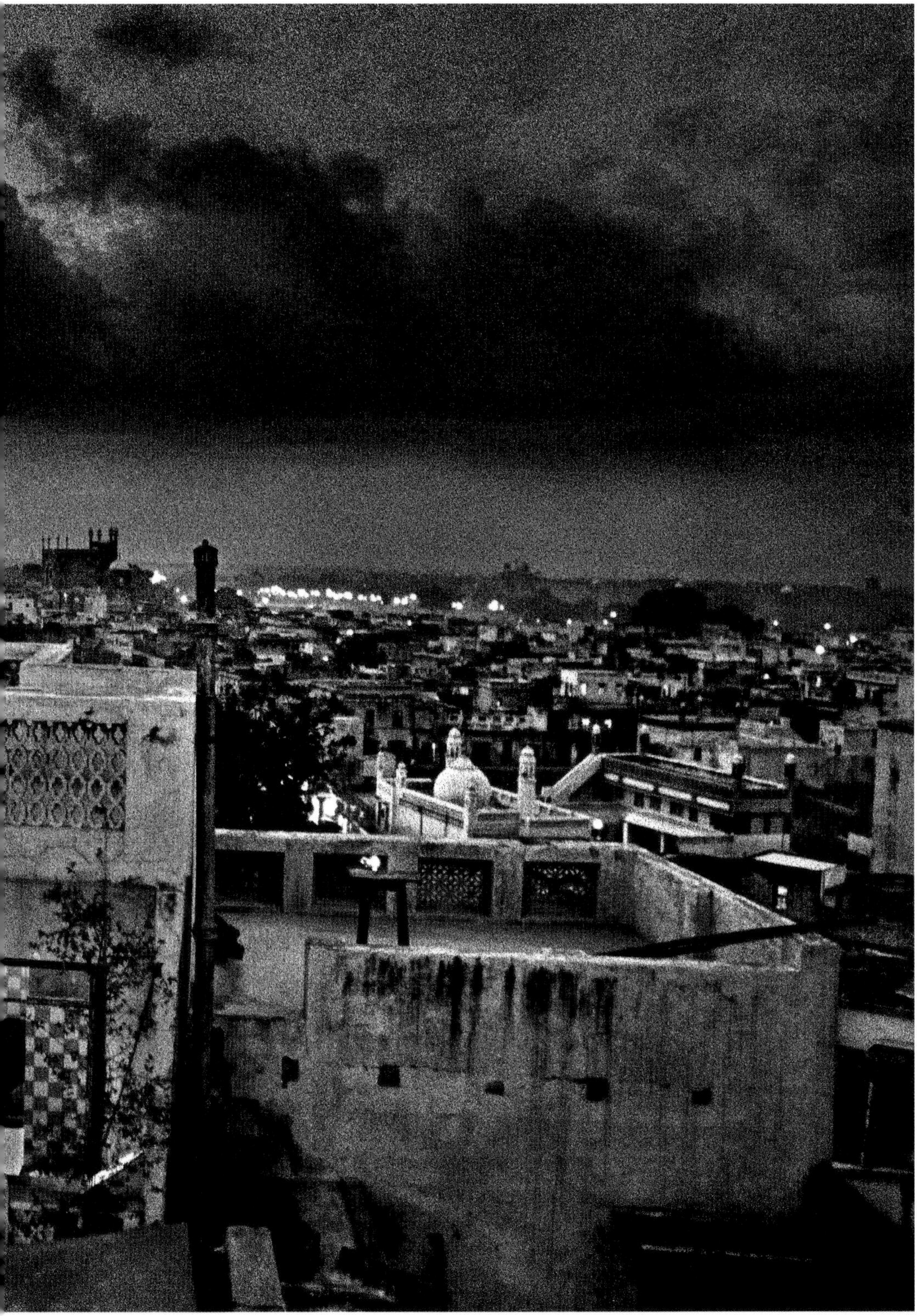

After the Durga Visarjan on the banks of the Hooghly in Kolkata, 1987

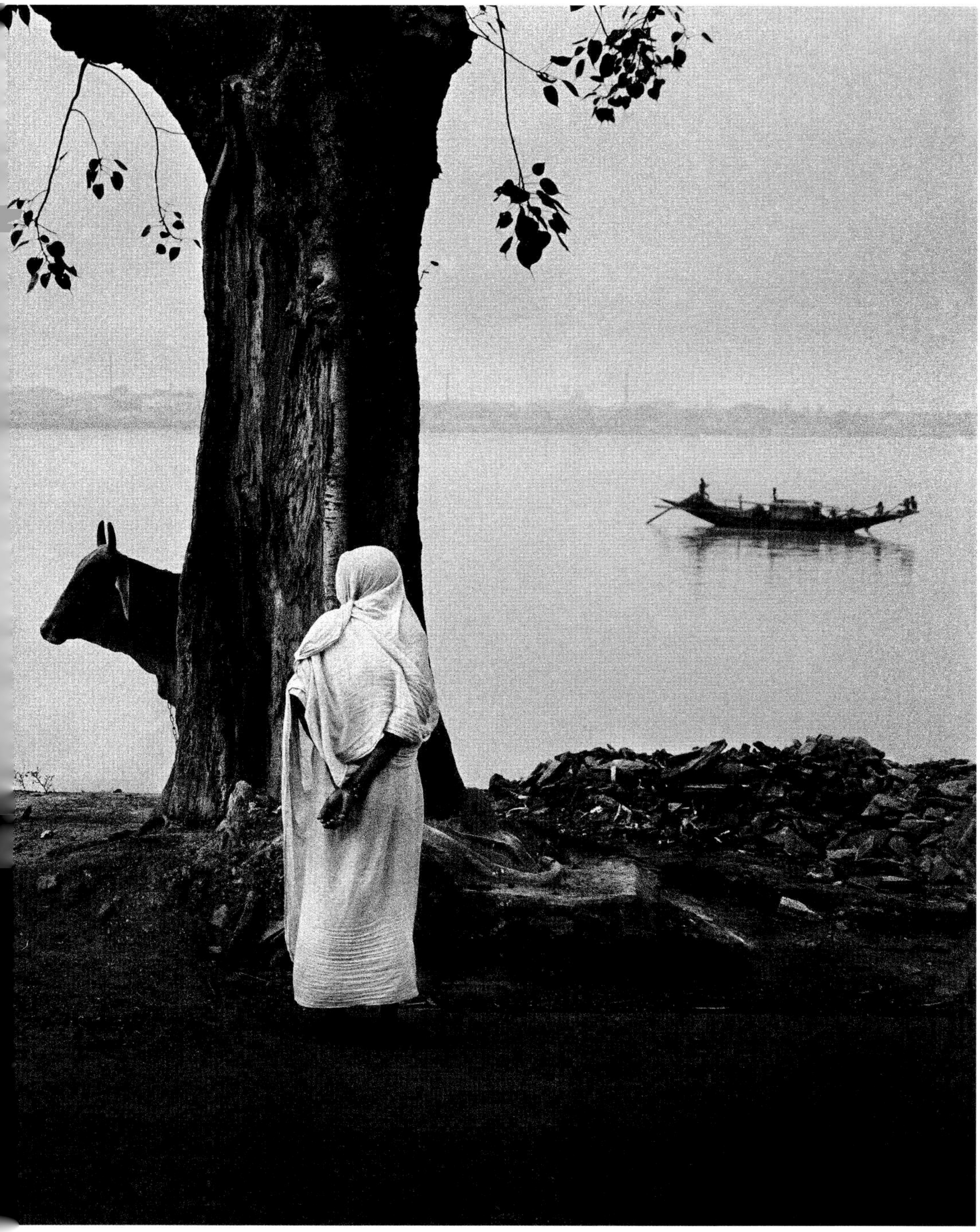

Morning rituals at Mulick Ghat, Kolkata, 1989

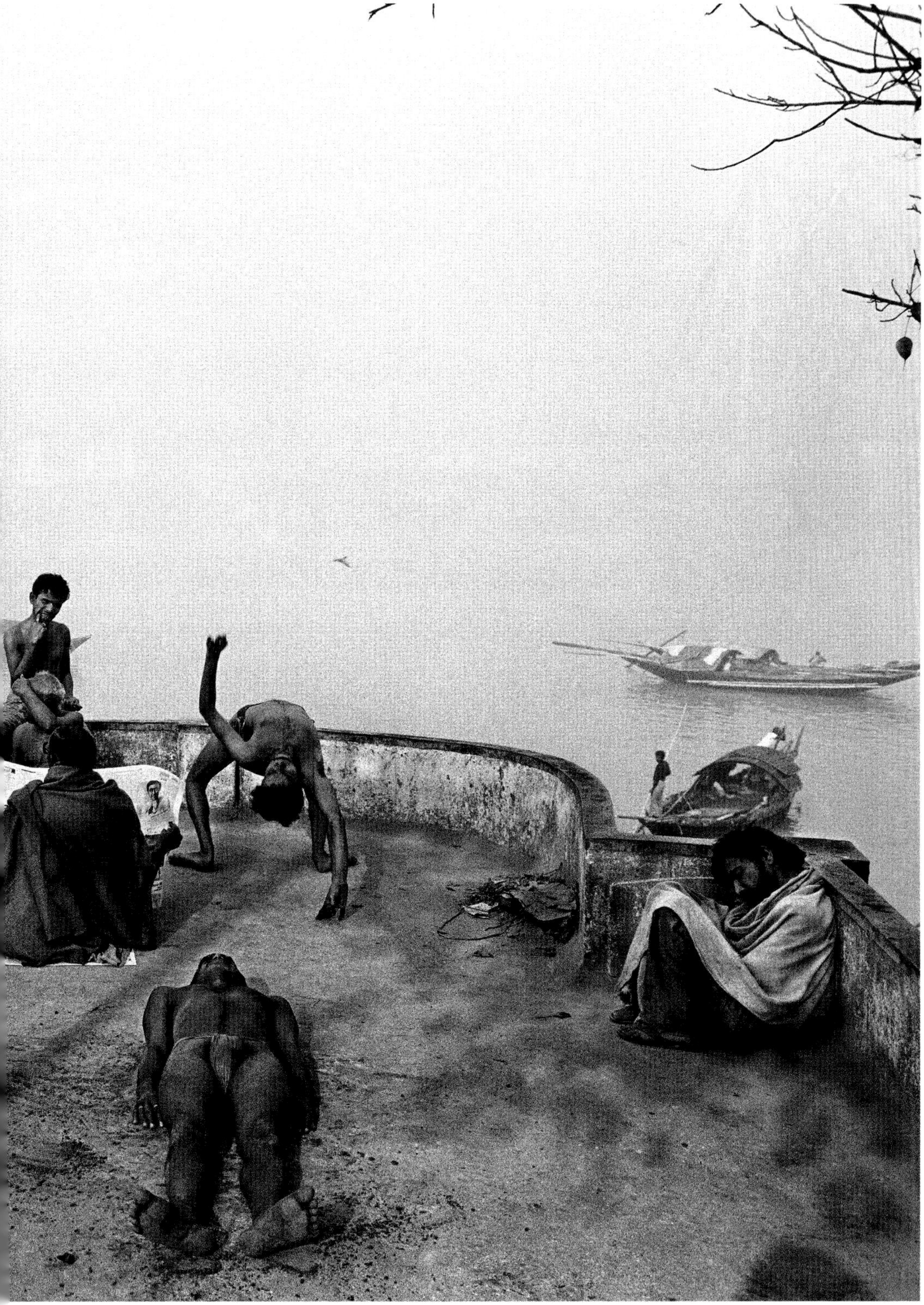

Relics of the past, 1992 At the Imambara in Lucknow, a magnificent monument from the Nawabi era that is now in ruins. The nonchalant young men lounging around exemplify our careless attitude to our priceless heritage.

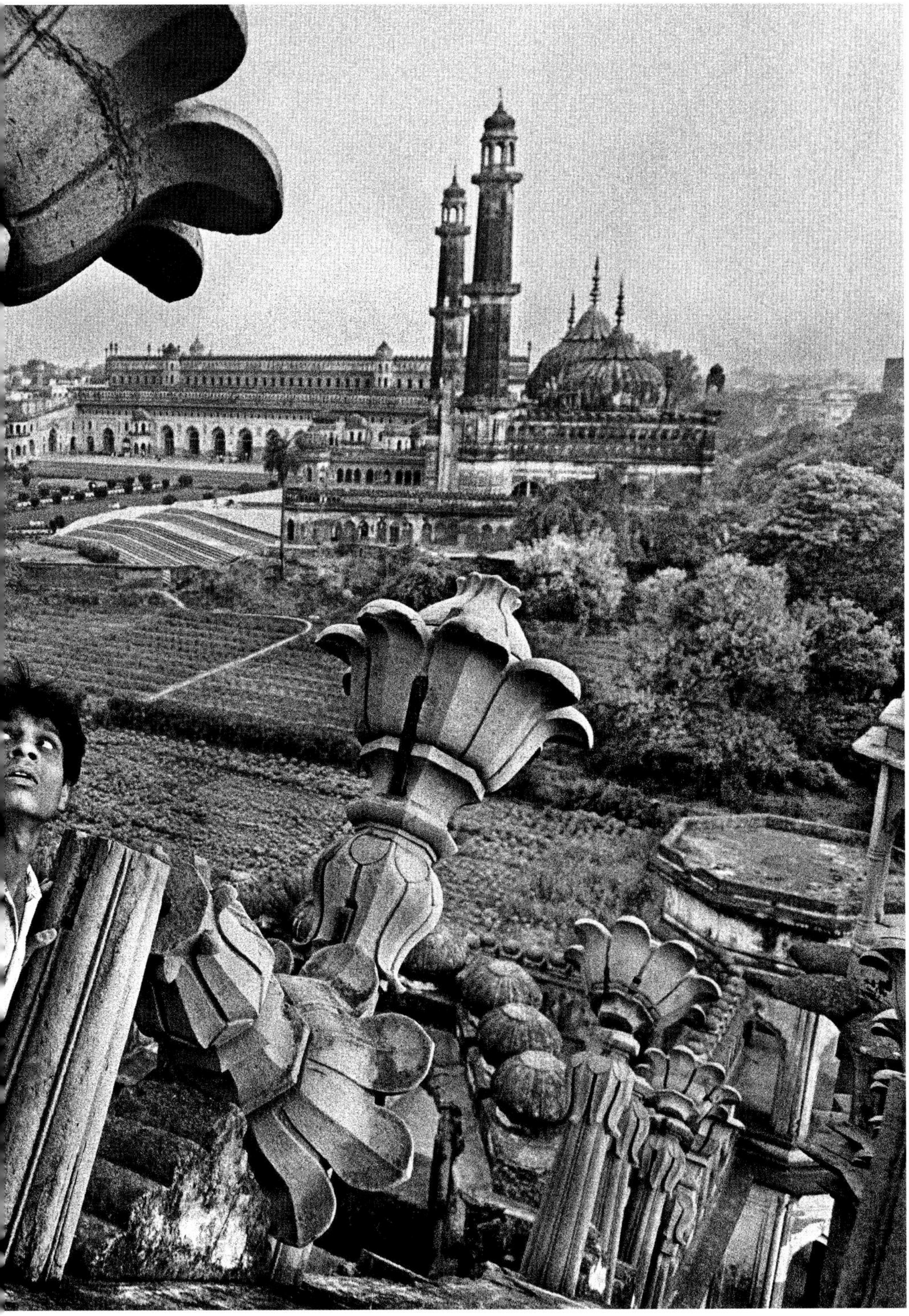

Monsoon downpour in Delhi, 1984

Modern India and the people who make it, 1982

PICTURING TIME | RAGHU RAI

Soft light and shadows in the mountains, 1982

Chaiwala, Delhi–Mumbai train, 1982

Portraits of a painter family, 1980

When I used to stay in Rabindra Nagar in New Delhi these people arrived to paint the house. There were two men from Rajasthan, and their wives and daughters—about six to seven people painting the house over five to six days. Each time I looked into their eyes—they were so much there as human beings. I felt very close to them and couldn't resist making them sit for pictures!

PICTURING TIME | RAGHU RAI

Above} His Holiness the Dalai Lama, 1975

Right} 1989

It was at the Kalachakra event that I first met the Dalai Lama. I photographed him from a distance for two days because he was sitting inside and we were never introduced. On the last day, when the initiations were over, Tavleen Singh, who was reporting for *The Statesman*, went to interview him and I took some portraits. Although it was my first encounter with him, he received me with the compassion and love that he bestows on everyone he meets. Today, I have the honour of being called his friend. When we meet, he hugs me and that is something unique and precious, it is a blessing.

PICTURING TIME | RAGHU RAI

Back in power, 1980

The people who ousted Mrs Gandhi from power could not hold on to their victory. Charan Singh was prime minister for 170 days before his government fell and mid-term polls were announced and Mrs Gandhi was voted back to power. Here she is, looking victorious, joyful and saintly. Ironically, in light of the events that would take place a few years later, the bulk of the people garlanding her are from the Sikh community.

PICTURING TIME | RAGHU RAI

Above} Bhindranwale at the Akal Takht, 1984

Right} After Operation Blue Star, 1984

I used to call him (Jarnail Singh Bhindranwale) paaji. To his followers, of course, he was a saint and they all called him 'sant ji'. Villagers and his devotees would visit him on the rooftop of the Akal Takht complex inside the Golden Temple. When they walked in they would throw down two rupees or five rupees, and after they'd gone he would pick up all the coins and notes and put them in his pocket. He was a small-minded leader who was made big by Giani Zail Singh and by a whole lot of ordinary Sikh farmers and villagers who didn't understand who he really was.

So one day two of his men came to my hotel at 11 o'clock at night. They said to me, 'Dekhiye, Jarnail ji jo ha i wo humare leader hai. Wo aapke "paaji" nahi hai. Aur aap unko paaji nahi bula sakte.' I said to them, 'Arre, unko bhi achha lagta hai, mujhe bhi achha lagta hai. To aapko kyun gussa aata hai?' With that 'warning' they went away.

Soon after, his goons began killing Hindus and Operation Blue Star was launched to put an end to his reign of terror. When things got too hot for him he took refuge inside the Akal Takht. I met him the day before he was shot dead. And he said 'Tu yahan kyon aaya hai?' and I said 'Arre paaji main aapse milne aaya. Main to aate hi raha hoon.' He asked, 'Ab kyon aaya hai tu?' I said, 'Dekhne ke liye ke aap kaise hai.' His eyes were bloodshot. There was anger and fear in them.

PICTURING TIME | RAGHU RAI

End of an era, 1984

On 31 October 1984, the invincible Indira Gandhi was assassinated by her bodyguards. A few days before her death, in an ominous speech, she had said, 'Attempts are being made to eliminate me. Every drop of my blood, I am sure, will contribute to the growth of this nation.'

Rajiv Gandhi (extreme left) against the rising flames at his mother's funeral, 1984

Above} Bhopal Gas Tragedy, 1984

A month after Mrs Gandhi's assassination, the biggest industrial disaster in India took place in Bhopal, when a leak at the Union Carbide Plant released deadly gas and chemicals killing thousands of people and permanently injuring thousands more. The next morning I was at the local Hamidia Hospital where the dead and affected were being brought in. The city had an eerie, post-apocalyptic atmosphere about it. At the cremation grounds, the Hindus were burning their dead and on the other side, Muslims were digging mass graves. Up to 10,000 people died within three days of the disaster. Thirty years on, the official death toll is 22,000.

Right} Burial of an unknown child, 1984

This haunting image came to symbolize the Bhopal Gas Tragedy in subsequent years.

PICTURING TIME | RAGHU RAI

Leonid Brezhnev, 1980

Brezhnev, the leader of the U.S.S.R., came to India when Indo-Soviet relations were at their peak. He looks like a stuffed dummy.

Zia ul Haq, 1987

This was a portrait for a *Time* magazine profile. Even though he's smiling, his evil spirit is reflected in the lines on his face and his sinister smile.

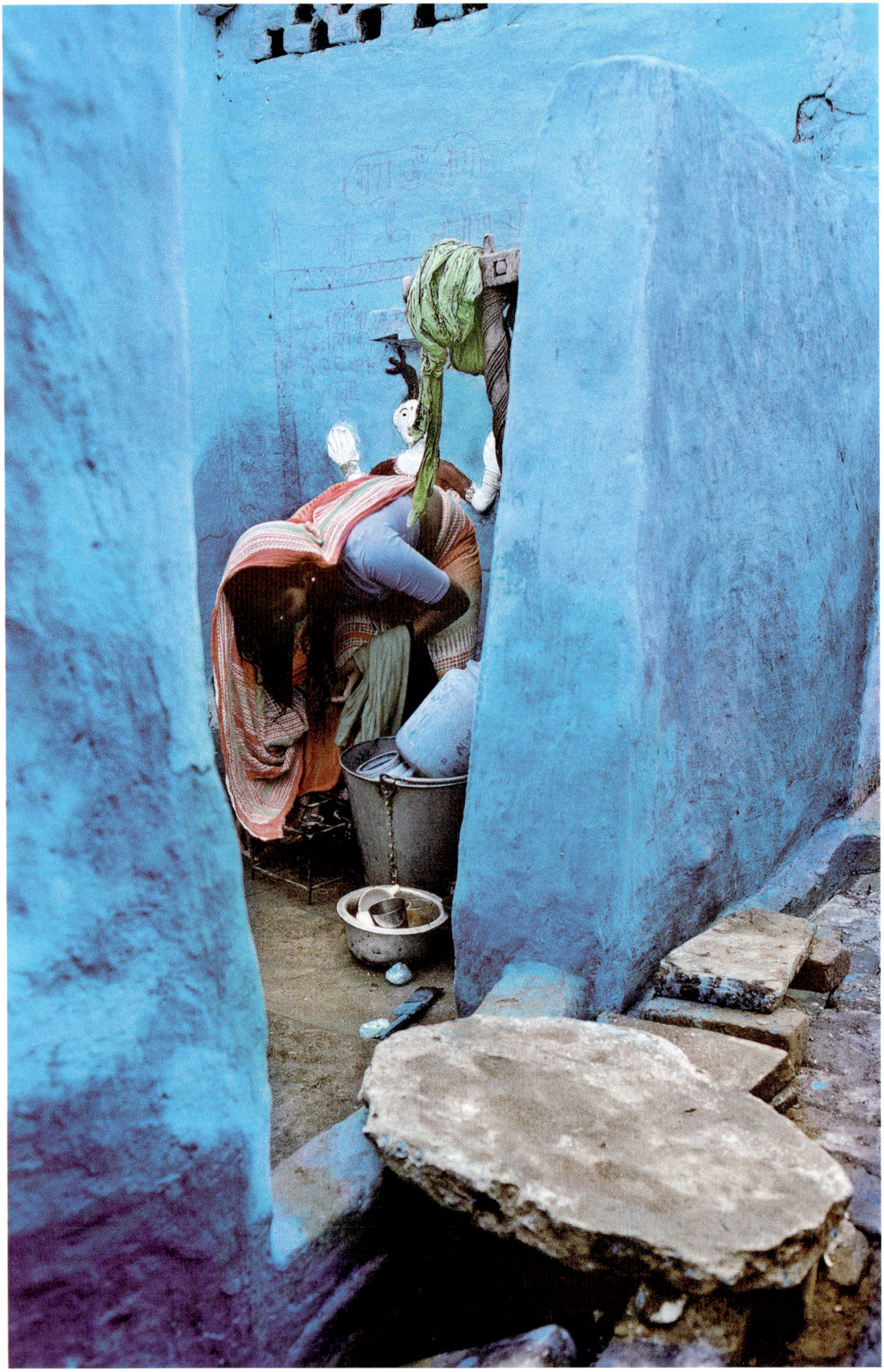

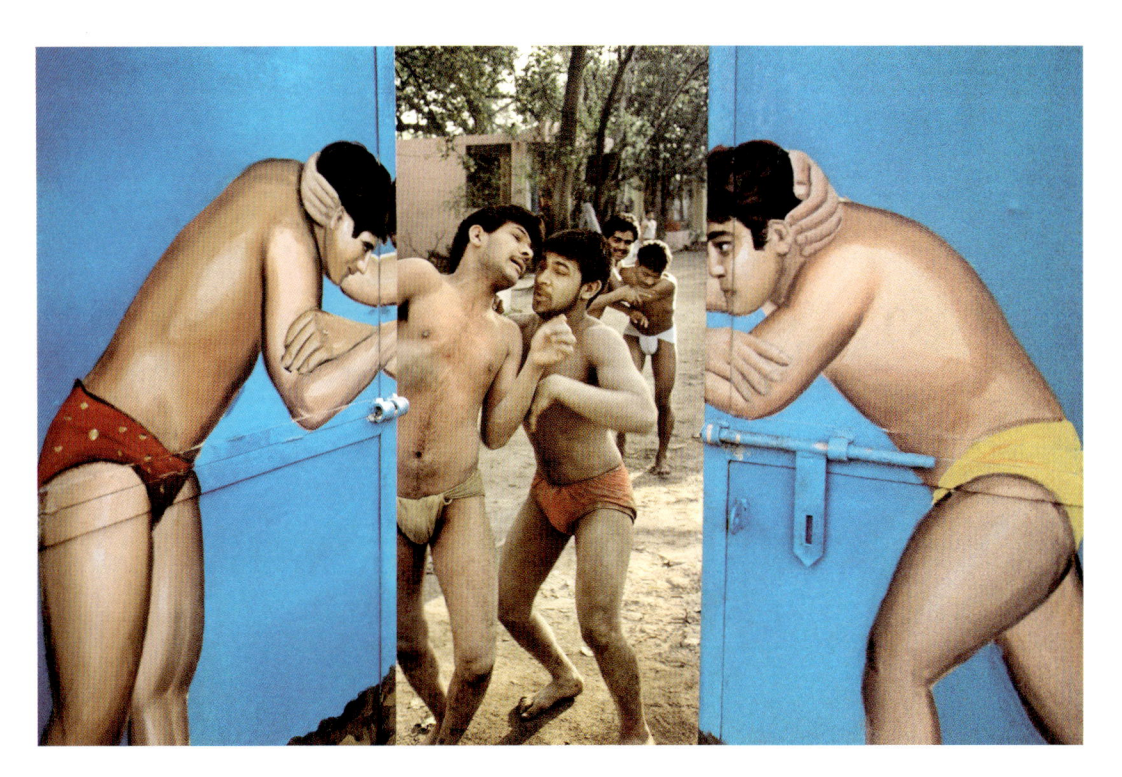

Above} Wrestlers at an akhara near Paharaganj, 1988

Left} Washing clothes, Gandhi Nagar, Delhi, 1989

Pre-monsoon clouds rise into a dust storm at Red Fort, 1986

I was carrying a medium-format camera that I had converted into a panoramic format. The storm was so strong that it was pushing us, I had spread my legs to stand my ground against the storm and with great difficulty I took a few pictures that captured the power of the storm.

PICTURING TIME | RAGHU RAI

Seagulls converging on the River Yamuna in Delhi, 1989

I was told by someone that a lot of migratory seagulls visit the Yamuna during winter. When I went, I saw hundreds of birds hovering around and they would swoop down towards this boat from which a man was feeding the birds. It turned out that this person was a businessman from Chandni Chowk, he had been coming to feed the birds since his father's time and had continued the tradition because it had brought prosperity to their business.

PICTURING TIME | RAGHU RAI

Pandit Ravi Shankar by the Ganga, 1986 This series of picture essays on classical musicians was something I started at *India Today*, and was a result of my deep love for classical music.

We began with Pandit Ravi Shankar, who was always a superstar.

Above} M.S. Subbulakshmi, 1987

When M.S. Subbulakshmi sang, she sang to the Lord. The intensity, dedication and passion was evident on her face.

Overleaf, Above} Hariprasad Chaurasia, 1988

Hariprasad Chaurasia's father was a well-known wrestler and he wanted his son to follow in his footsteps, but his love for music won.

Overleaf, Below} S. Balachander, 1988

S. Balachander playing the veena in Mahabalipuram. The notes he played (and his voice) were very deep, resonating. When I heard it, I was reminded of a huge rock vibrating in perfect rhythm, so I took him to Mahabalipuram to photograph him amidst these seventh-century boulders.

Overleaf, right} Ustad Bismillah Khan, 1988

Ustad Bismillah Khan, the shehnai maestro, was a very gentle, wonderful human being. Towards the end of his life, the pressures of providing for his large extended family robbed him of peace and contentment.

Bhimsen Joshi, 1986

PICTURING TIME | RAGHU RAI

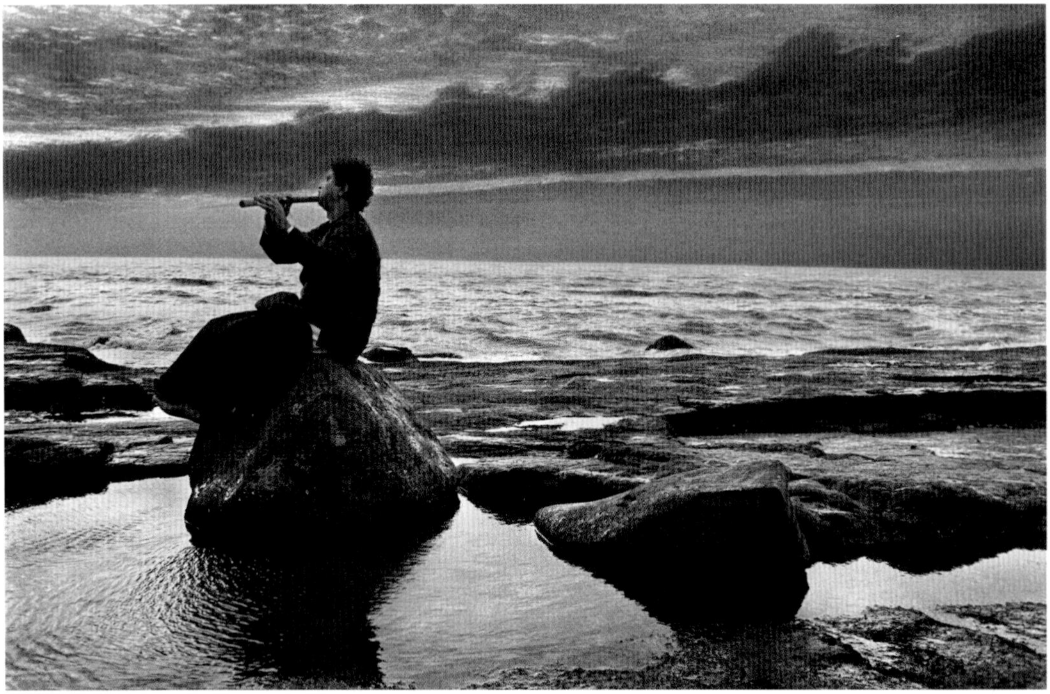

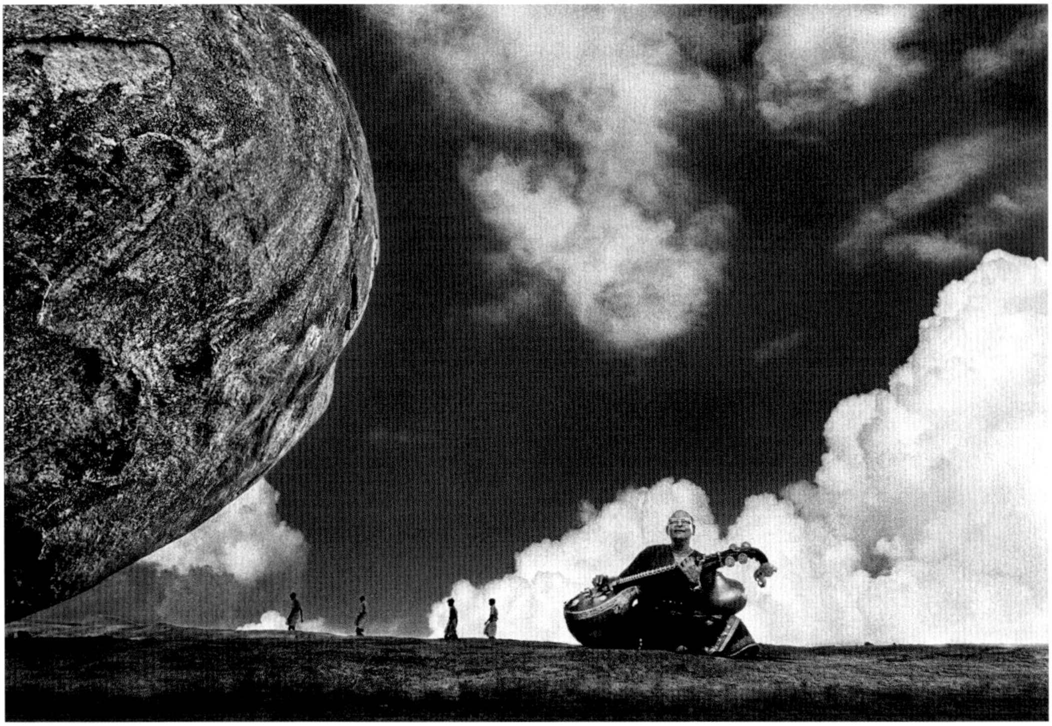

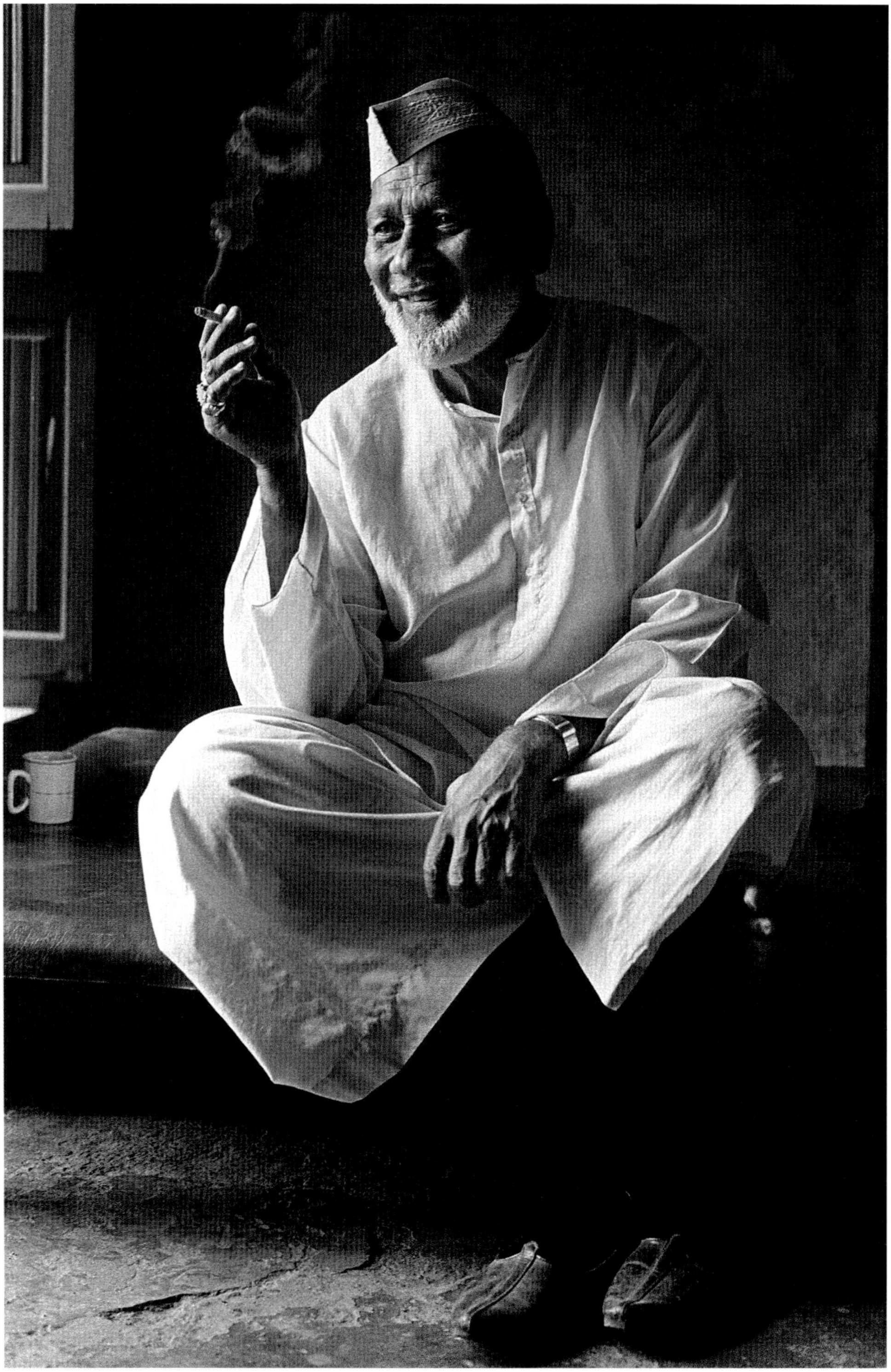

Satyajit Ray, 1989

Satyajit Ray on location for his film *Ghare Baire*. We had a great equation based on mutual respect and admiration for each other's work.

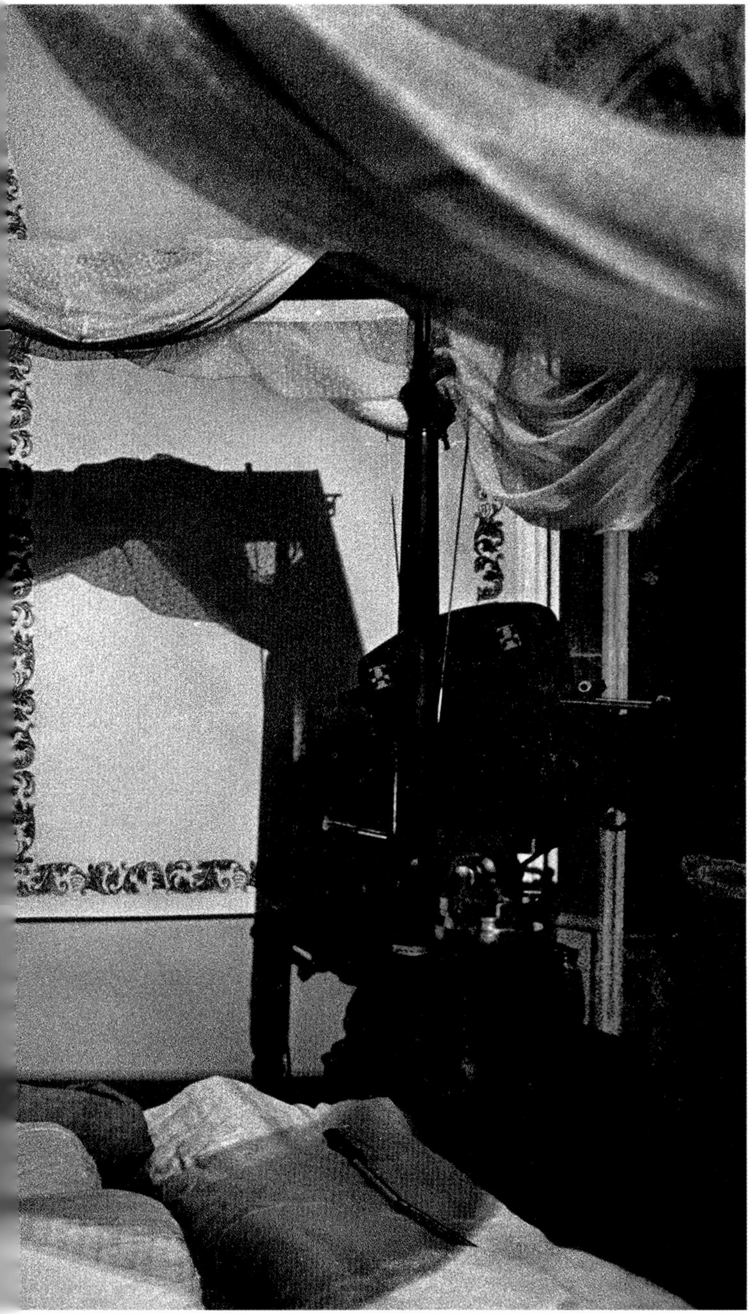

1990s

On seeing the post-apocalyptic sight of Ayodhya after the Babri Masjid demolition and riots, I realized that human beings can become monstrous and extremely destructive in the name of religion. During this period, I also undertook several international projects. And though I was a home bird I would readily travel for assignments. The death of Mother Teresa was a sad day in our lives. Her dedication to the cause of working for others was inspiring and it resonated with me, and with millions. Yet another tragedy struck the country in the form of the Kargil war.

~

Ayodhya, 1992 The town was a picture of calm a day before the demolition of the Babri Masjid. It was hard to believe that this same place would be witness to extreme violence in a few hours.

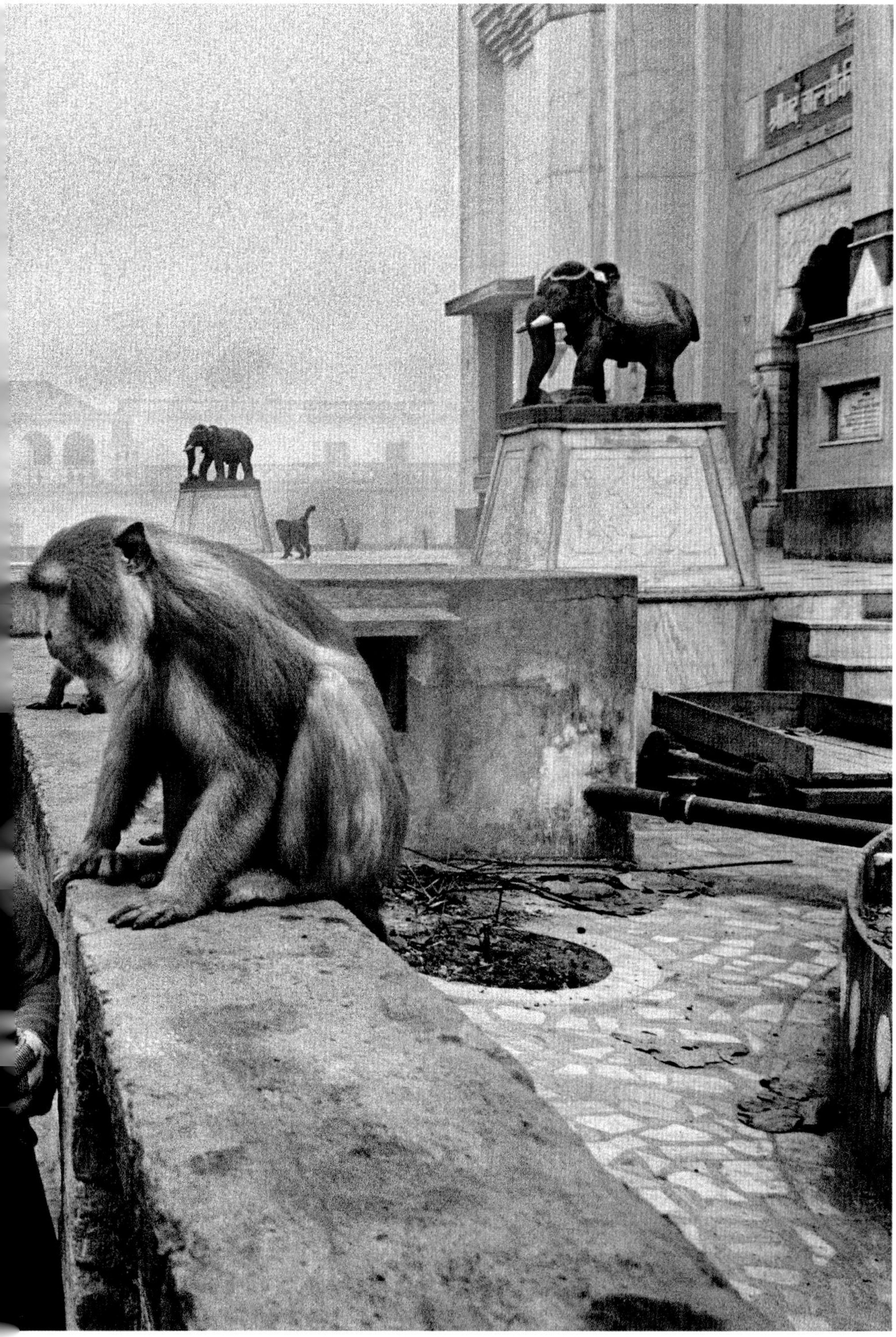

Ayodhya, 1992

The day after the Babri Masjid was demolished, paramilitary forces were deployed to prevent untoward incidents. The leaders of the ruling party were accused of dereliction of duty and not doing much to prevent the tension from spreading.

PICTURING TIME | RAGHU RAI

PICTURING TIME | RAGHU RAI

Congress session in Tirupati, 1992

Manmohan Singh at the All India Congress committee session when he was finance minister in the P. V. Narasimha Rao government. The Congress's sycophantic tradition of putting up larger than life pictures of its leaders lends this picture a prophetic meaning.

Mother Teresa, 1995

Mother was around eighty-five when I took this picture. With time, Mother was more 'connected' when she folded her hands for prayer.

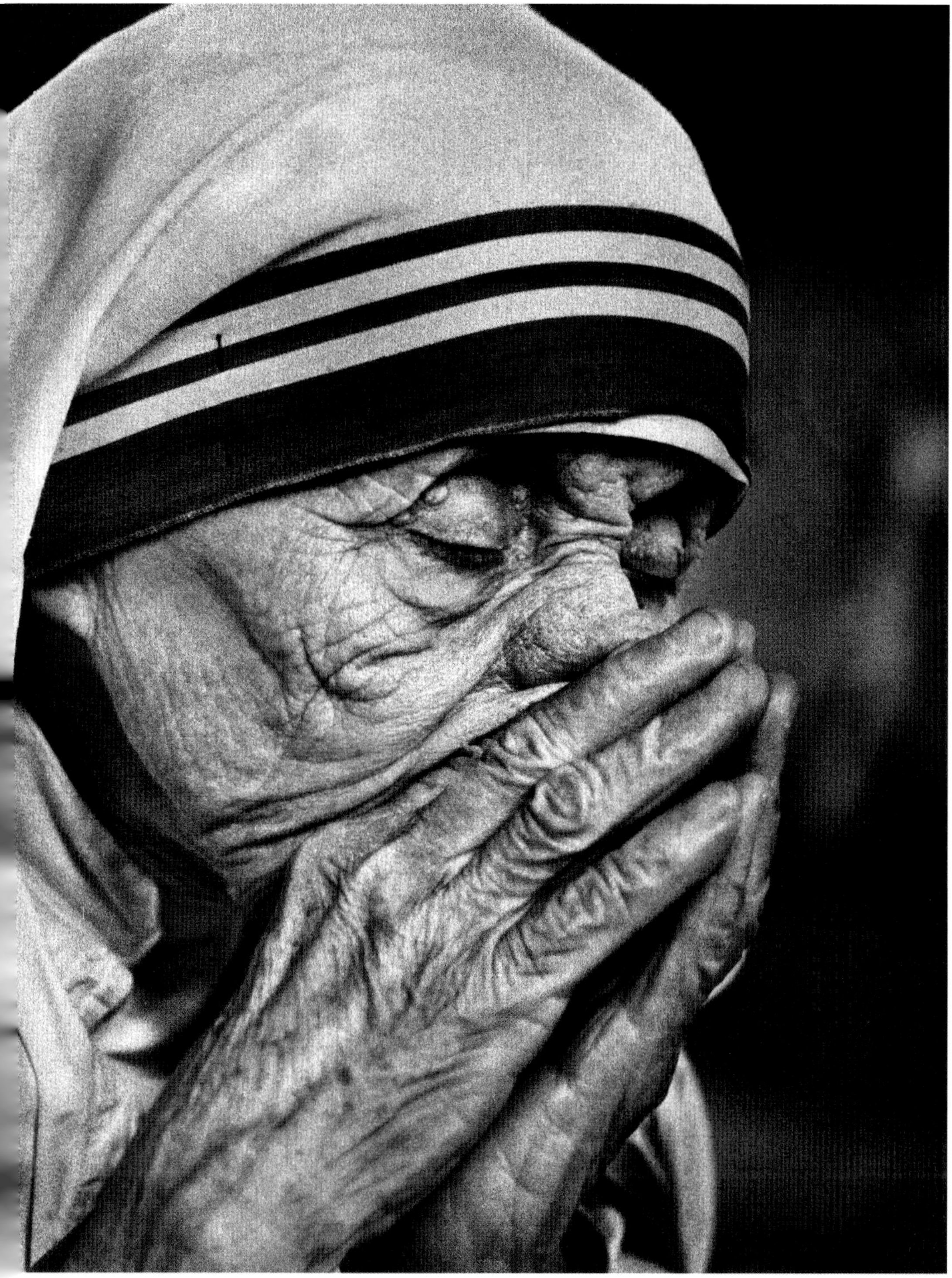

His Holiness the Dalai Lama, 1993

This picture was taken for *Time* magazine on the rooftop of his palace. It was a rainy and cold afternoon. He was wrapping a shawl around himself and I shot a few quick pictures.

A few years later, he turned to me and asked in his honest and childlike way, 'How do I look after my surgery?' And I replied, 'Your Holiness you look as handsome and strong as the Himalayas.'

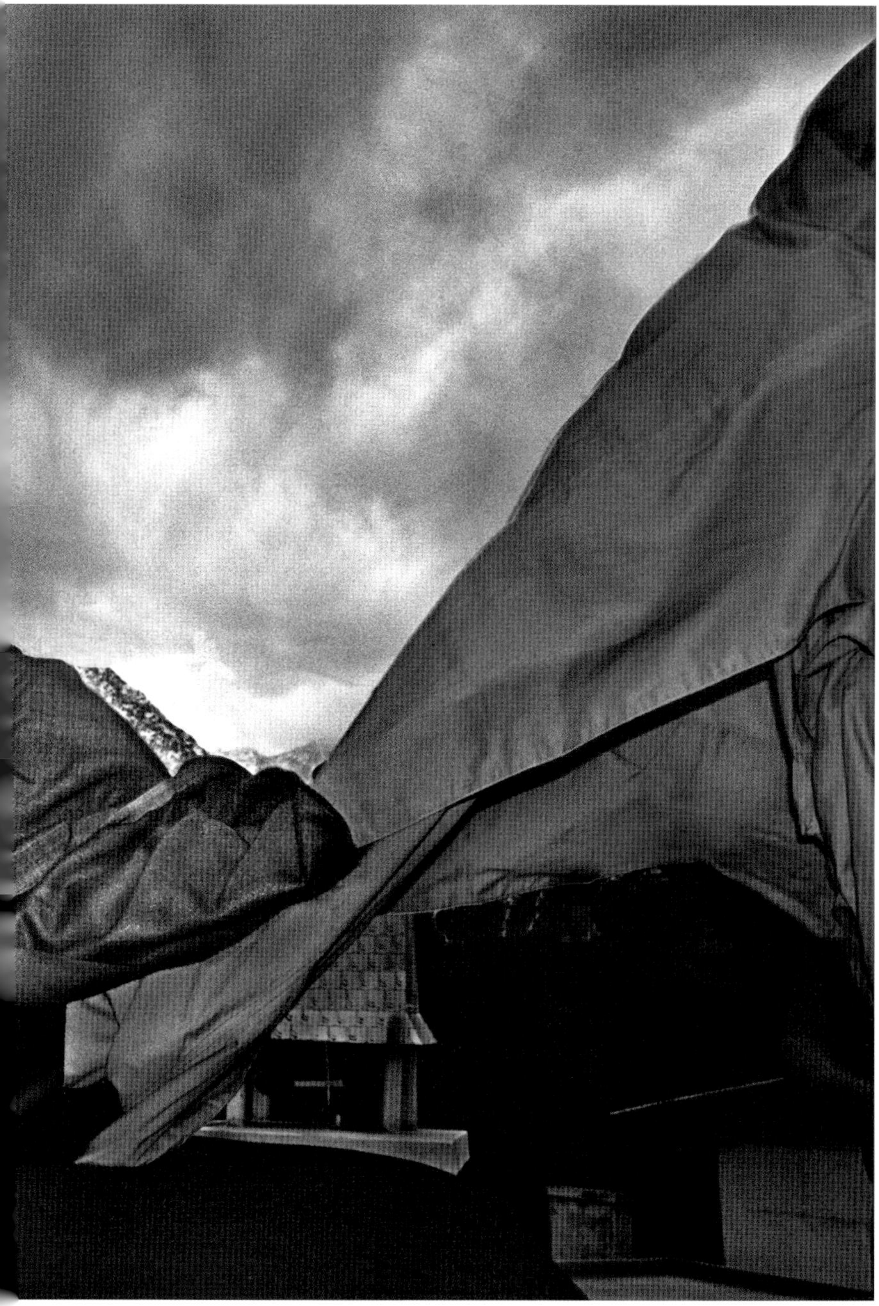

A spiritual quiet, Mexico, 1999

Paris, 1998

In 1998, *Le Figaro,* the French newspaper, had invited six photographers from around the world to photograph Paris. I took this picture of a mime performance in front of the Sacre Coeur church.

Fall of the Soviet Union, Moscow, 1991

Jerusalem, 1994

Toy train to Darjeeling, 1996

I was doing a story on the toy train to Darjeeling. This picture is special to me because it is four dimensional—scenes from the right, left, front, and back, all in a single frame.

Churchgate Railway Station, Mumbai, 1996

Local trains are the lifeline of Mumbai. The platform is a sea of humanity—one minute, it is bursting with people, the next minute, as the train pulls out, the deluge is over. I was mesmerized. To capture this human deluge, I had to put my camera on a pole, and set it for long exposure so it would capture the energy that was overflowing. I went from one platform to another looking for my picture before I came across these three men calmly sitting and reading their newspapers.

Kargil, 1999

The day after I went up to photograph the war, a ceasefire was declared. I was able to take these pictures of the Indian army with Bofors guns.

PICTURING TIME | RAGHU RAI

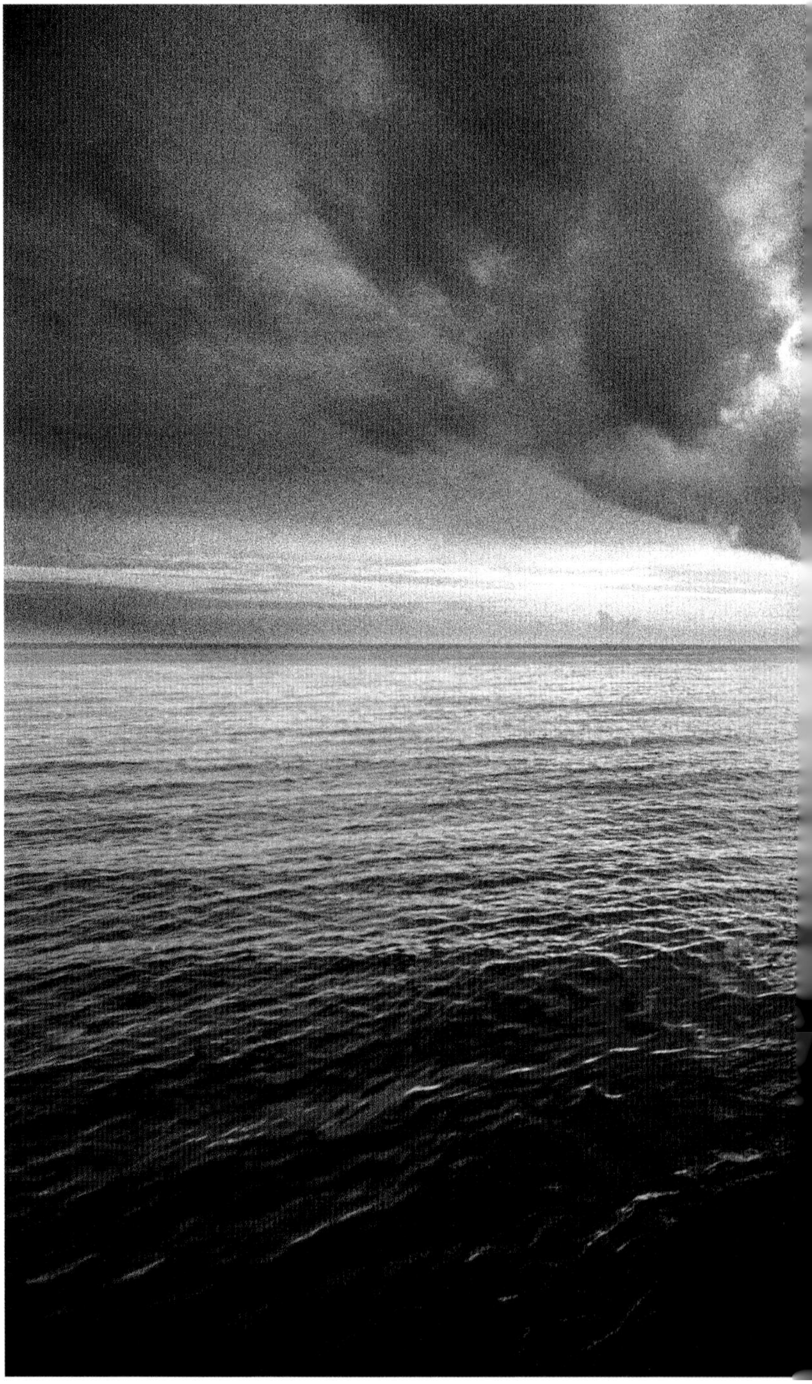

Monsoon in Mumbai, 1994

This was late in the evening, intense clouds were looming over the city. These people on the edge of Marine Drive look as if they are searching for something.

Mango trees near Haridwar, 1996

My father was a circle superintendent with the Punjab irrigation department and my childhood was spent near canals. Growing up there were mango orchards and other plantations all around us. I came across these mango groves on my way to Haridwar and they instantly transported me to my childhood.

Manikarnika Ghat, 1994 Manikarnika Ghat in Varanasi, a strange, enigmatic place where people from across the country come to cremate their dead in the hope that they will attain Nirvana.

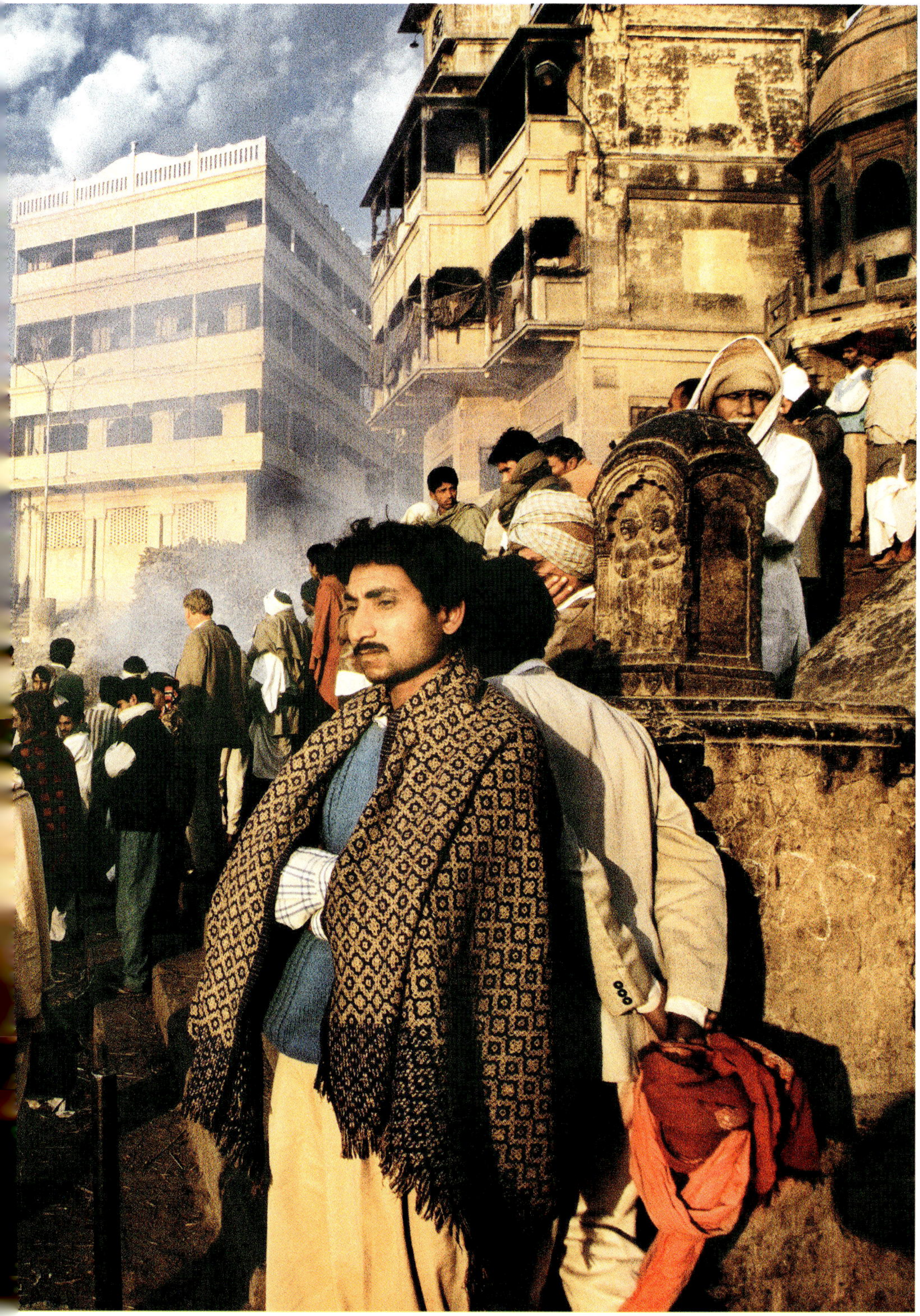

On a beach in Mahabalipuram, 1995

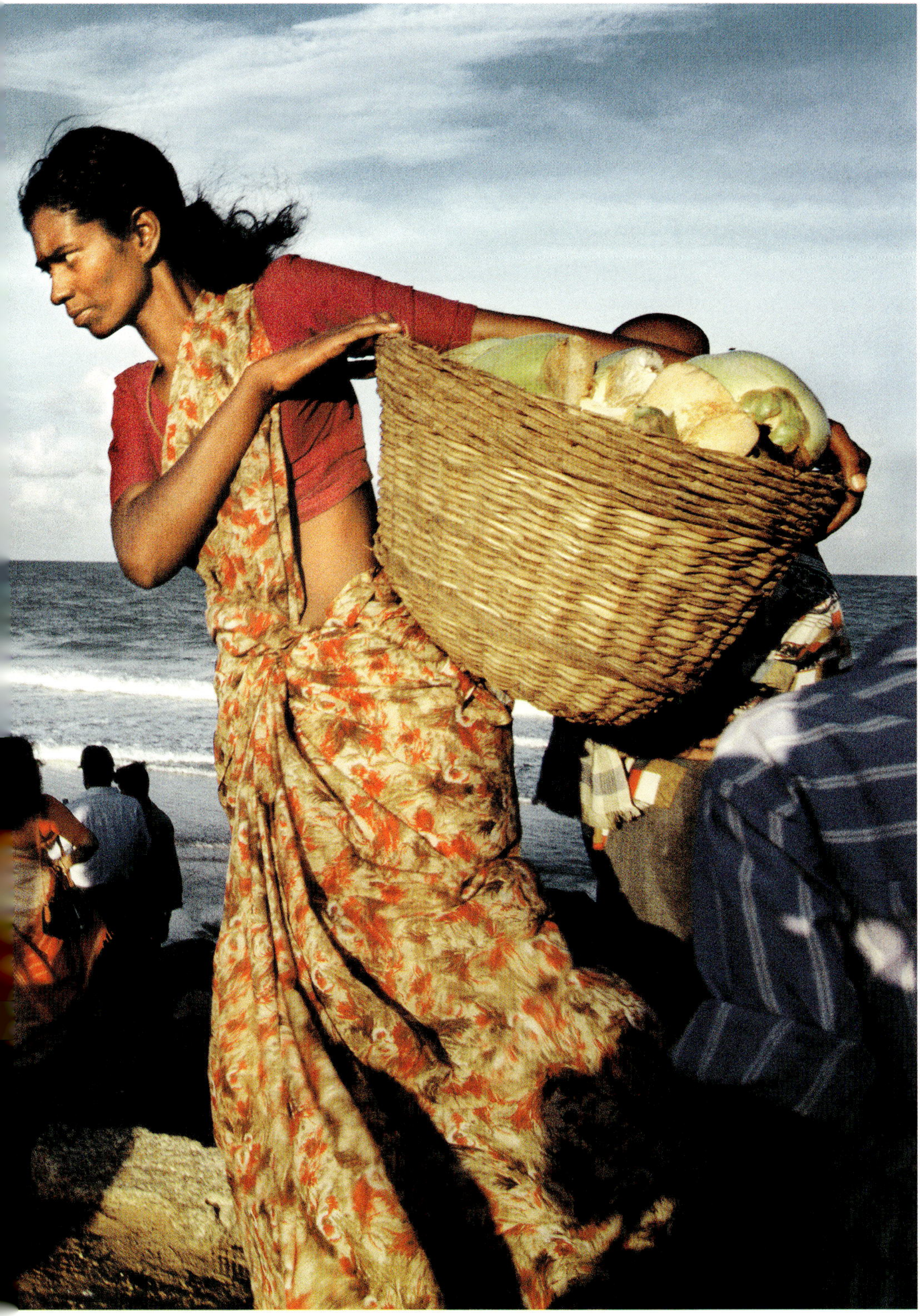

132
133

Cow at Kandla Port, Gujarat, 1996

This cow is having a whale of a time eating fresh wheat.

2000s

In these pictures, I've tried to capture the essence of the country's different towns and cities. I found Kolkata and Varanasi to be the most expressive cities of the country which overflow with human expression all the time. The mighty Himalayas in Ladakh are absolutely mesmerizing—each time you take a turn, the forms the textures acquire different colours. Then there is Mumbai and its powerful people who enthrall you with their stories.

~

Ganesh Visarjan in Mumbai, 2002 There is so much energy in the atmosphere. Even the splendid clouds look like they're bidding farewell to Lord Ganesh.

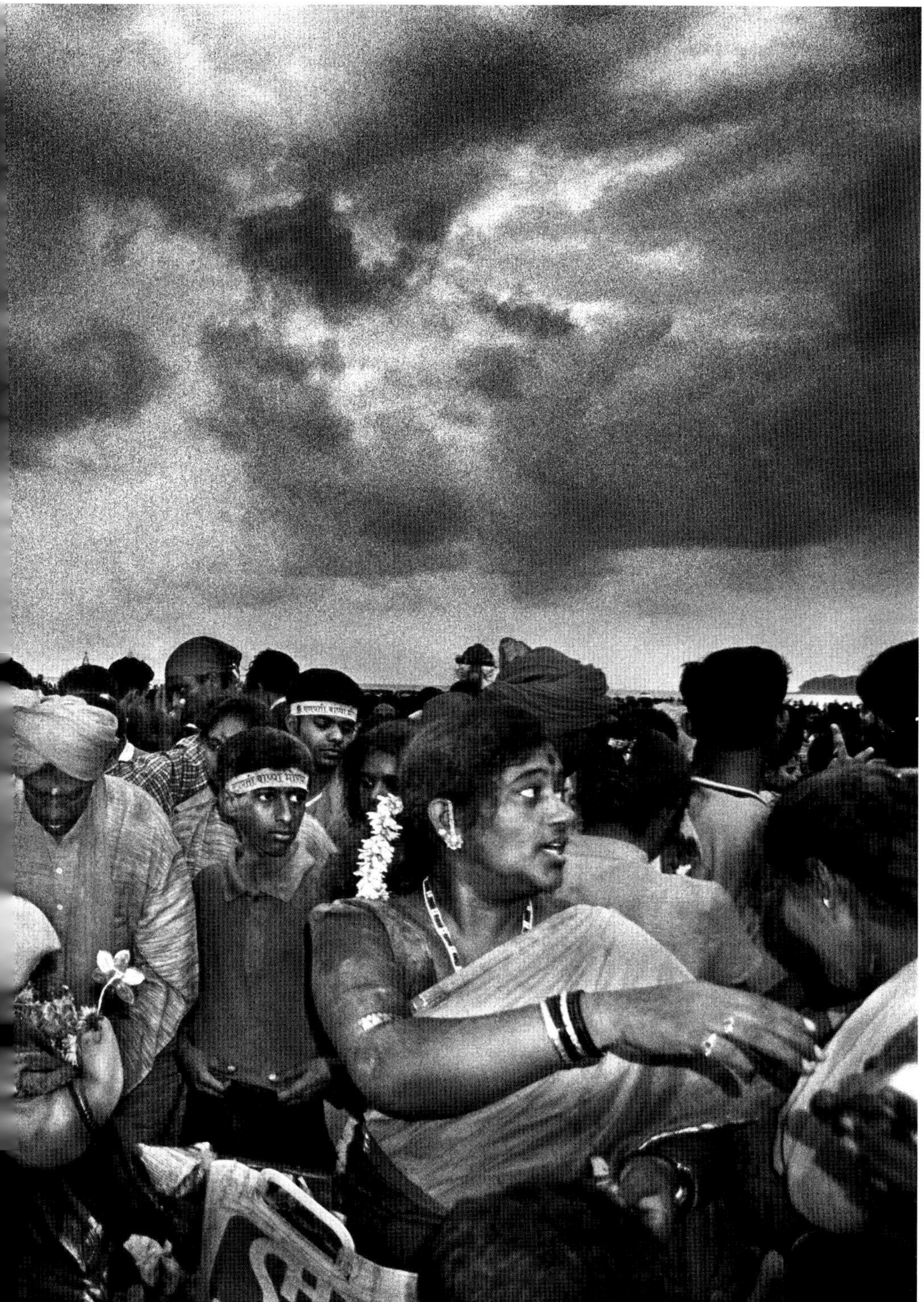

Visitors at Kanyakumari, 2006

Kanyakumari is very precious to me because being the southernmost point of India it is literally the 'charan', the feet of my Motherland.

PICTURING TIME | RAGHU RAI

Wrestling akhara at Babughat, Kolkata, 2004

It was a display of bodies and limbs, mirrored in the form of the trees and their roots.

PICTURING TIME | RAGHU RAI

Men holding a rope on a construction site, 2000

This picture personifies Mumbai in a lot of ways. The sea and the hills in the background, sky-high buildings, and these men constructing another mighty structure; this is the essence of the city.

The cacophony of a Kolkata street, 2004

Migrant labour have a strong presence in Kolkata.

Portrait of Bal Thackeray, 2002

I expected Bal Thackeray to be a brusque and intimidating man, but he was rather friendly. About two hours into our shoot, at noon, he informed me that it was time for his wine and cigar. His glass was somewhere close by, and without any pretension he posed with his cigar for my camera.

PICTURING TIME | RAGHU RAI

Varanasi, 2007

Varanasi is one of the very few important holy towns in this country. One feels the presence of the divine in every corner, every object.

PICTURING TIME | RAGHU RAI

PICTURING TIME | RAGHU RAI

Sadhu in Allahabad at Kumbh Mela, 2001

Woman in a meditative trance, Varanasi, 2008

Kumartuli in Kolkata, 2009

Although Kolkata is gradually urbanizing, some parts such as Kumartuli still exude the charm of a bygone era.

The artisans of Kumartuli are the force behind the intricate Durga idols that are at the heart of the Durga Puja celebrations that grip the city every year for ten days.

PICTURING TIME | RAGHU RAI

Artist's studio in Kumartuli, Kolkata, 2004

An artist's studio in Pal, near Kumartuli. Today, it's a storehouse of sculptures and busts of Tagore, Vivekananda, as well as international leaders like Kennedy and Stalin, and ordinary men and women. These sculptures are so lifelike that when you walk in you feel as if you are in the presence of these great people.

PICTURING TIME | RAGHU RAI

Akshardham Temple, 2005

I've never seen another Hindu temple of this scale and craftsmanship in recent times.

PICTURING TIME | RAGHU RAI

Mornings in Varanasi, 1976

A young girl in her free-spirited moments, 2006

Marine Drive, Mumbai, 2008

I keep looking for things that symbolize the
cities I visit. And the sea is symbolic of Mumbai.

Children selling flowers at Marine Drive during the
late evening, 2008

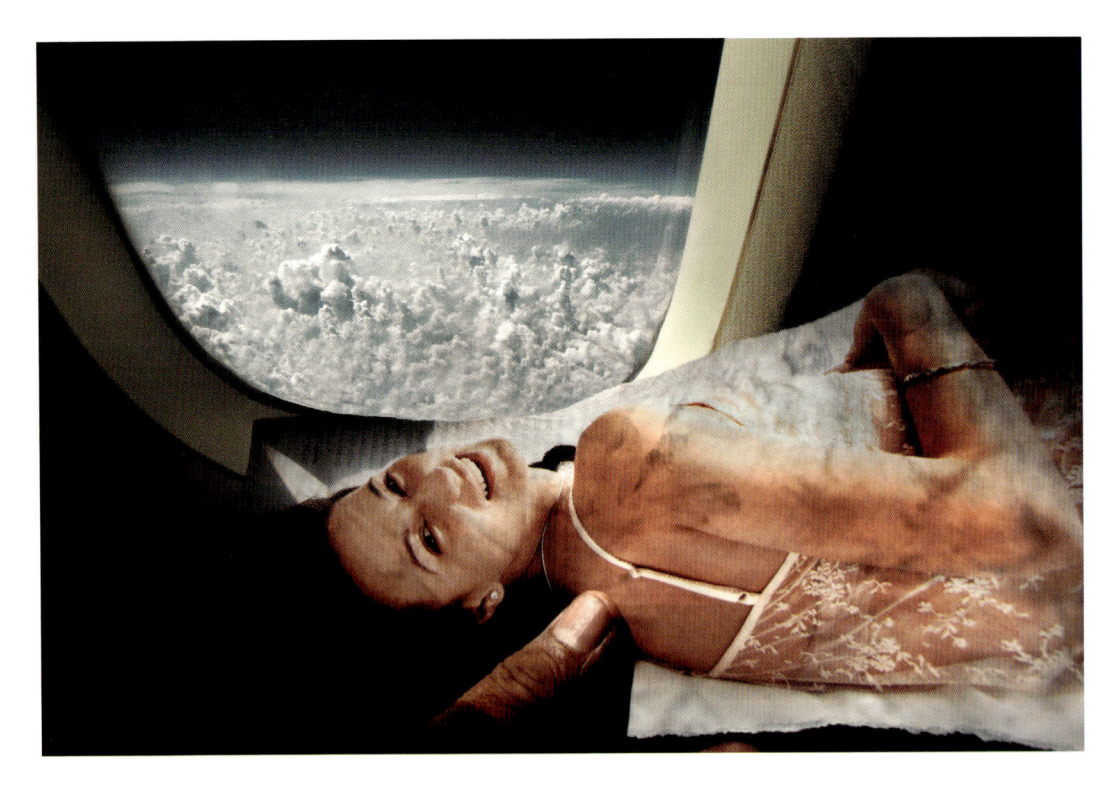

Up in the air, 2009

I love clouds. Since I couldn't jump out of the plane and dive into them, I decided to try and use them in a photograph. I blended these photographs of dreamy-looking women in a glossy magazine with the sunshine streaming in through the window, and the clouds outside. The inside blended with the outside.

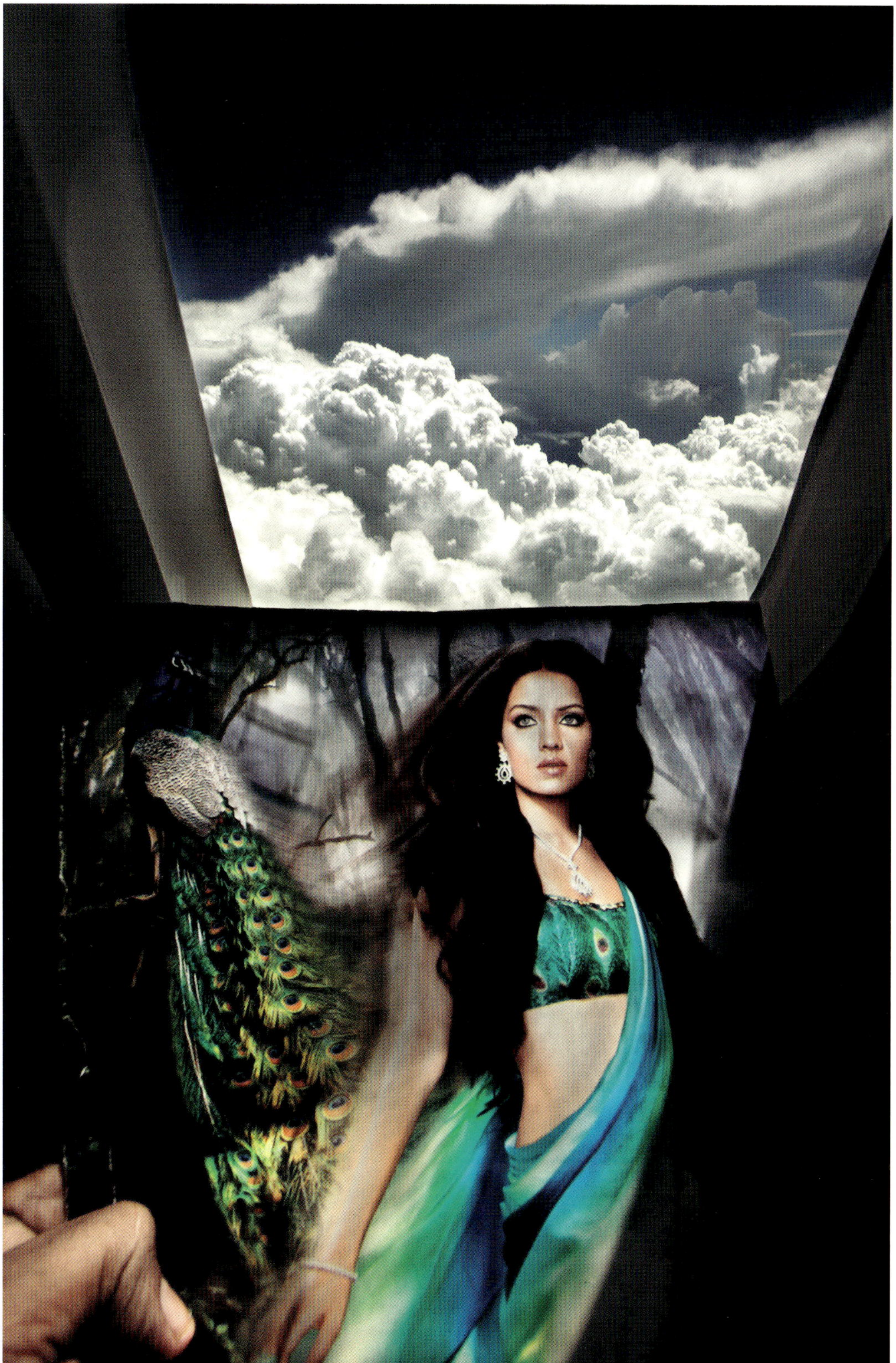

2010s

Creative people are a product of their own personal journeys—of explorations and meditative pursuits where even small experiences and little nuances have their own edge and importance. When I look back at the past five decades, I feel a sense of wonder and amazement. These moments were gifted to me by nature and
I caught them...

~

Family holiday in Goa, 2010 The setting was perfect—it was getting dark, the clouds were intensifying, there was a stranded ship near the shore (which I thought I could hijack).

River Brahmaputra, Arunachal Pradesh, 2011

Maheshwar Ghat in Madhya Pradesh, 2011

This was when River Narmada was flooding and it was constantly drizzling. I couldn't protect my lens anymore,

Beach in Mahabalipuram and Jantar Mantar in Jaipur, 2015

These dark clouds charge me up and they add an extra dimension to my life.

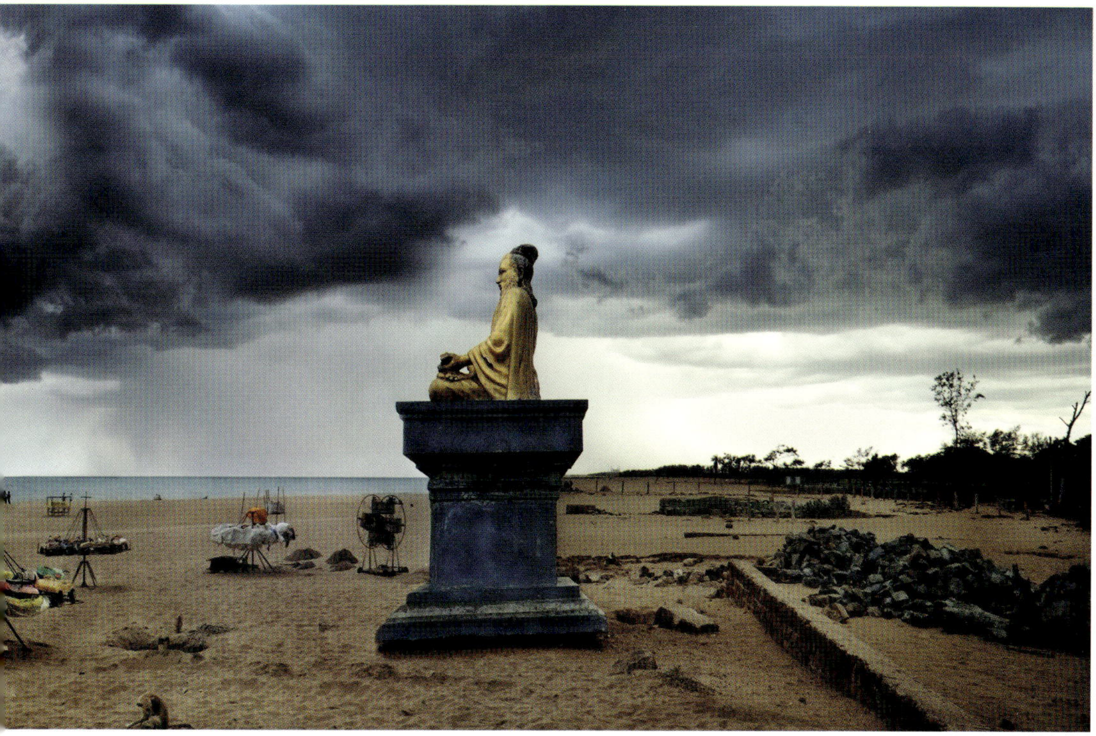

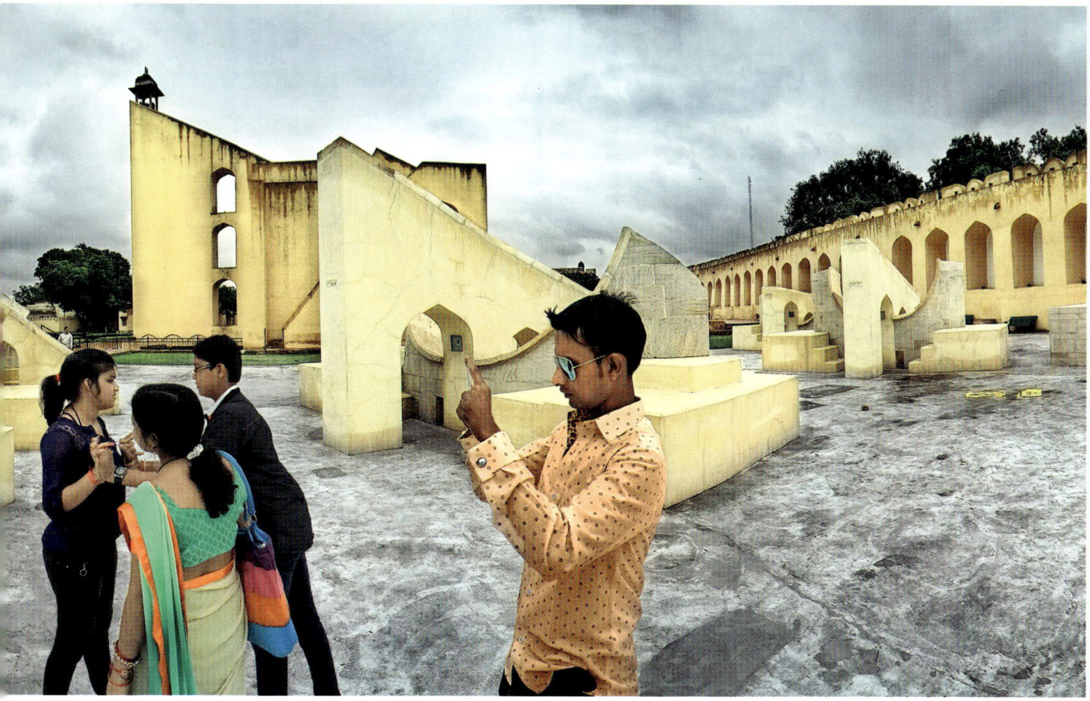

Backdrop series in Rajasthan, 2010

Little ladies of Kutch pose for a picture.

Desert women, flawlessly colourful and beautiful.

Sadhus at Mahakumbh, 2013

Naga sadhus of the Juna Akhara at prayer.

Naga sadhus, 2013

After taking a holy dip in the cold waters of the Ganga, these Naga sadhus smoke a chillum to warm themselves.

Leh, Ladakh, 2014

His Holiness the Dalai Lama and monks scientifically preparing a mandala for the Kalachakra initiation ceremony.

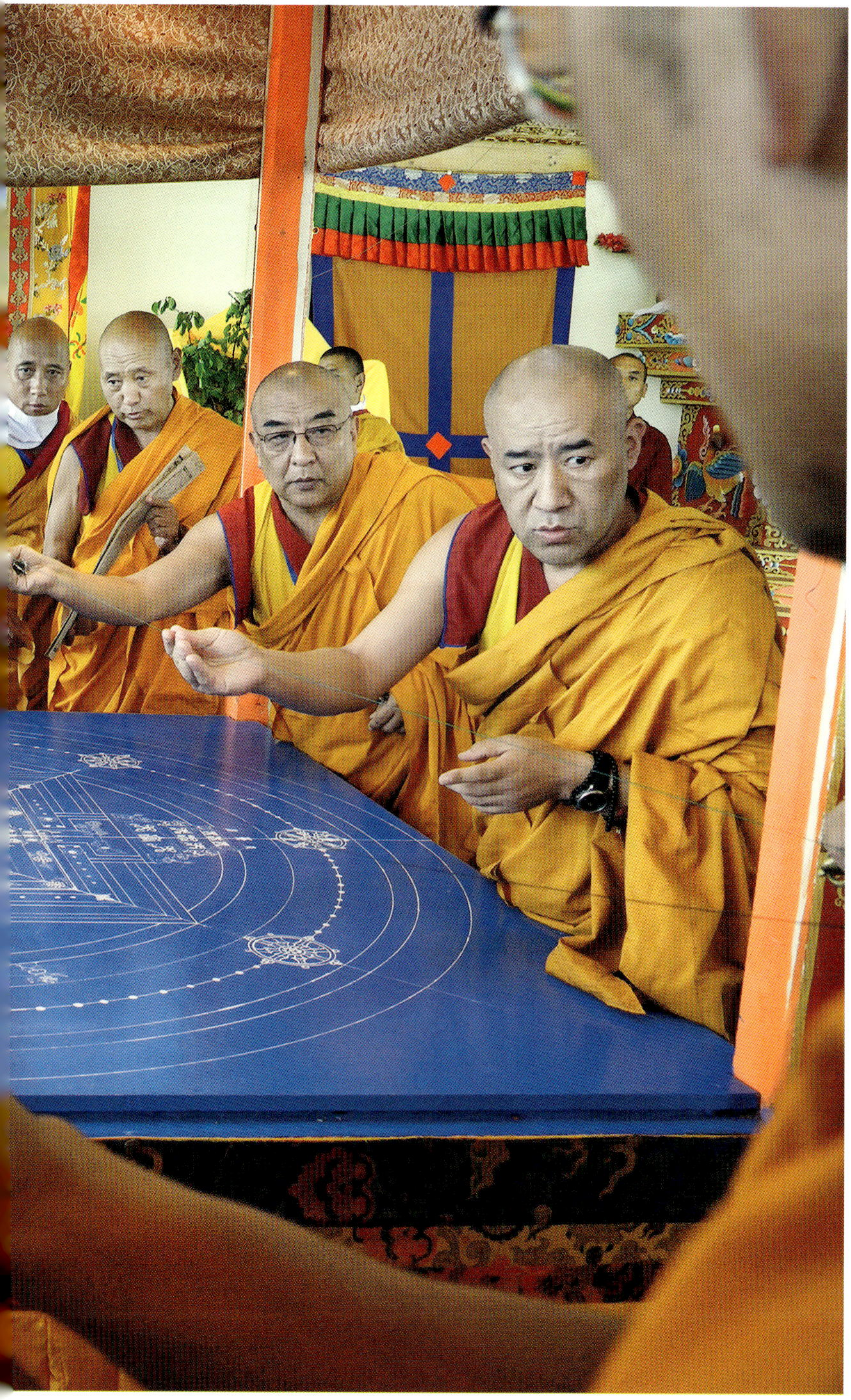

Right, Above} From the 'Trees' series, 2014

Right, Below} Hampi, 2012

I was dining with a friend at a small restaurant in Hampi across from this rock. That is when I saw the shadow of the tree on the rock; the sight of the shadow moving was a spiritual experience. Post lunch, I went and slept on this rock to complete my experience.

PICTURING TIME | RAGHU RAI

Above and Overleaf} Stone boulders in Hampi, Karnataka, 2012

The experience of being with nature—especially the Hampi rocks, and how almost every time the monsoon clouds would cast a shadow in the skies—is an extraordinary feeling. No lens can quite capture its expansiveness and power.

I discovered that the Roundshot camera can literally capture 360 degrees in one go. And that camera created the magic.

PICTURING TIME | RAGHU RAI

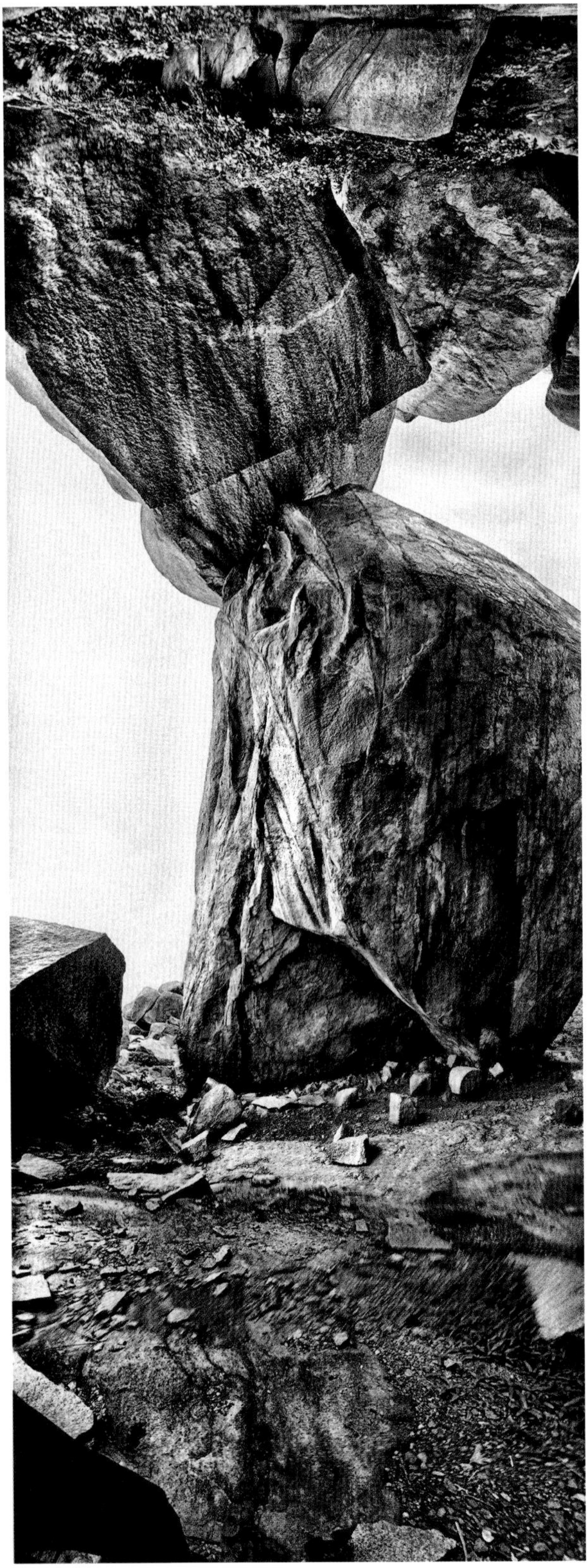

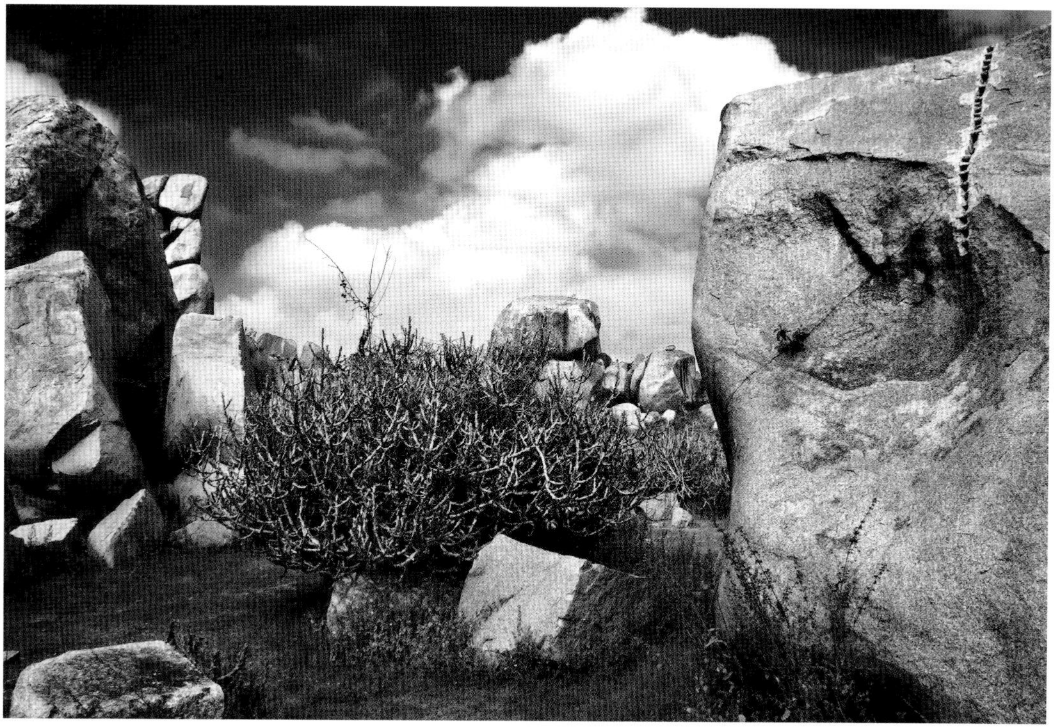

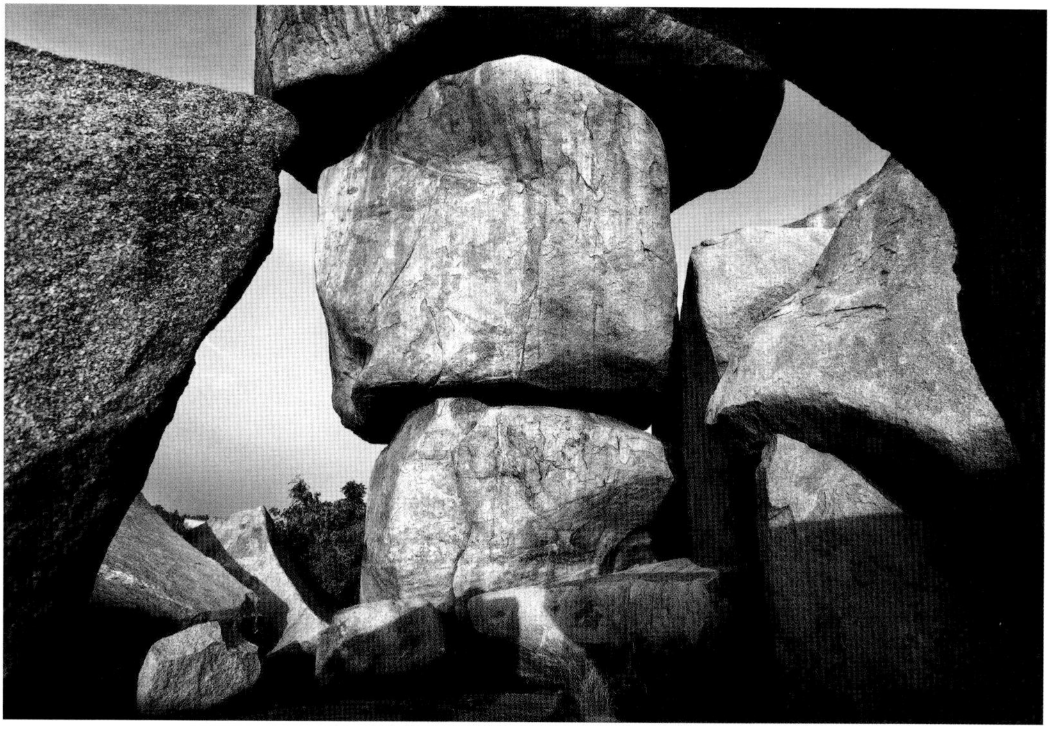

View of the Lamayuru Monastery, Ladakh, 2000 The Lamayuru Monastery is on a hilltop in Ladakh at an altitude of 11,552 feet. While it looks as though a mighty rainstorm could wash it downhill, this mysteriously perched monastery actually dates back to the tenth century.

Surreal landscape, Ladakh, 2014

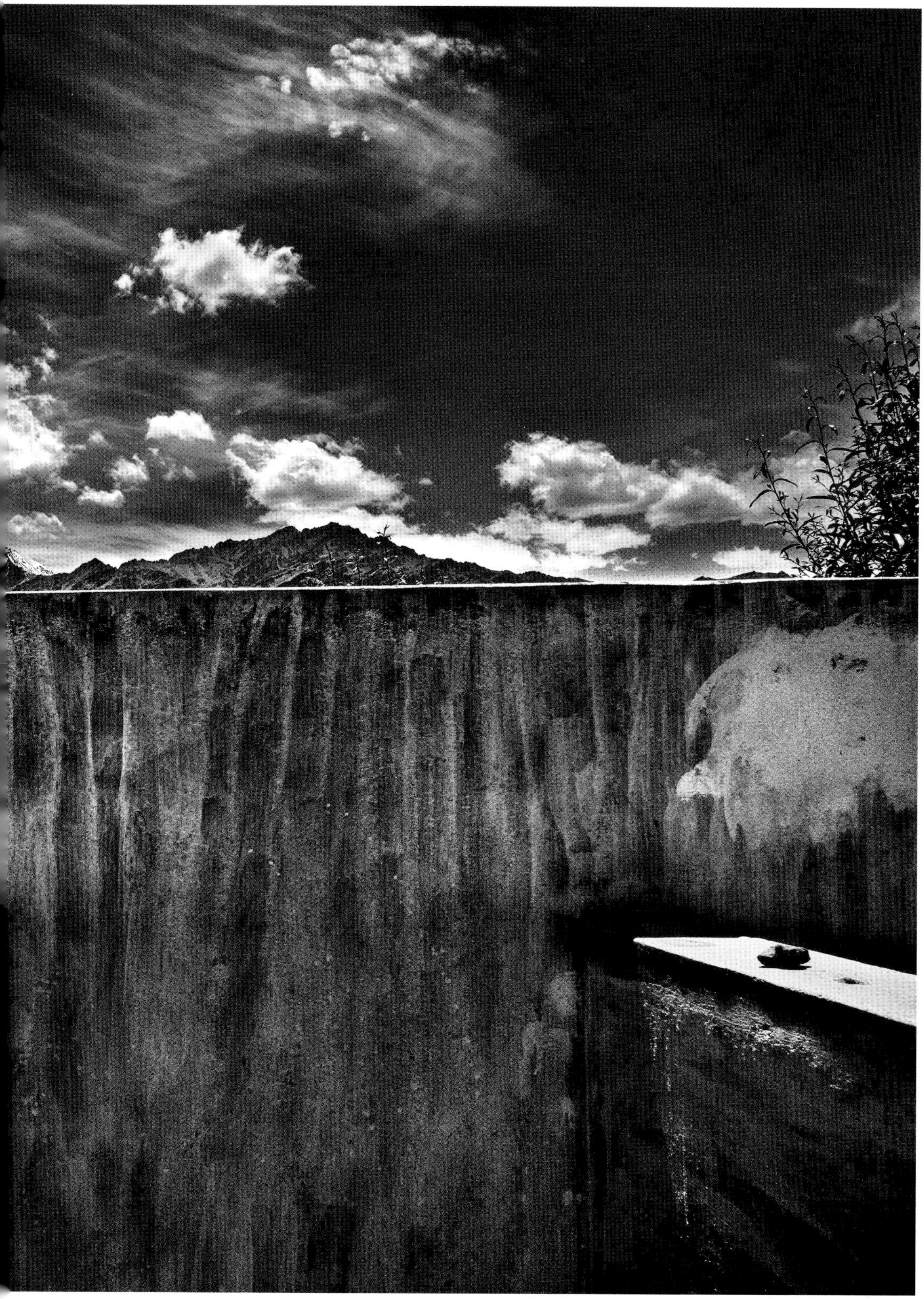

The spirit of light that touches us and the space around us in a moment of silence, Ladakh, 2014

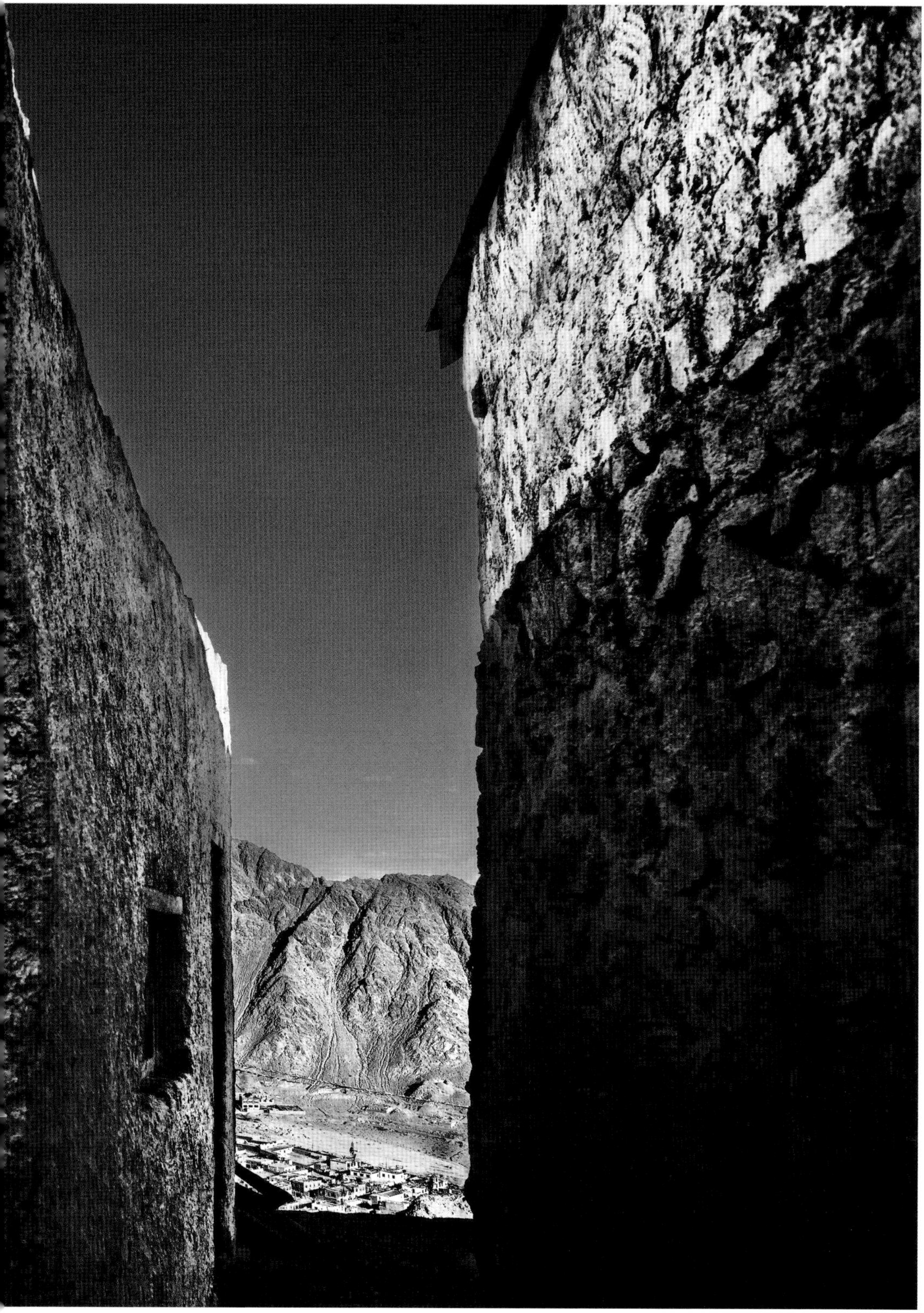

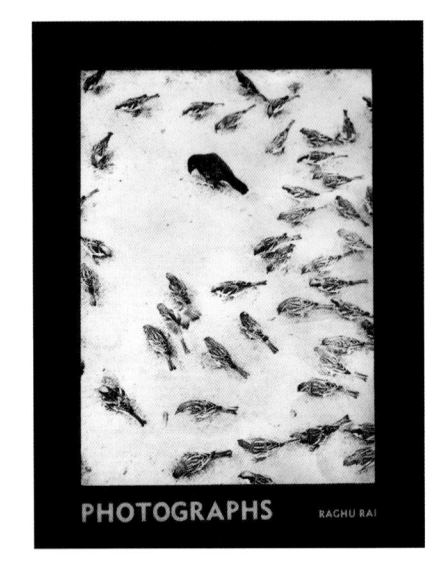

The catalogue of my first exhibition, 1969

Books by Raghu Rai

Gujarat
Vijayanagara Empire: Ruins to Resurrection
The Tale of Two: An Outgoing and an Incoming Prime Minister
Trees: Whispers
Bangladesh: The Price of Freedom
The Indians: Portraits From My Album
India's Great Masters: A Photographic Journey into the Heart of Classical Music
Varanasi: Portrait of a Civilization
Mother Teresa: A Life of Dedication
Raghu Rai's India—Reflections in Colour
Raghu Rai's India—Reflections in Black and White
Indira Gandhi: A Living Legacy
Exposure: Portrait of a Corporate Crime
Raghu Rai's India—A Retrospective
Lakshadweep
Calcutta
Taj Mahal
The Sikhs
Delhi
A Day in the Life of Indira Gandhi

Books co-authored by Raghu Rai

Mahakumbh: A Spectacle of Divine Design
Bombay—Mumbai: Where Dreams Don't Die
Raghu Rai's Delhi
Khajuraho
Tibet in Exile
Romance of India
Indira Gandhi

In Jhang, 1987 I visited my birthplace to a warm and moving reception. This photograph was taken by my friend Saeed Naqvi.

Timeline

1942:	Born in Jhang, Punjab (now in Pakistan)
1965:	First job as a photographer, *Hindustan Times*
1966-76:	Chief photographer, *The Statesman*
1971:	Published his first book, *Indira Gandhi**
	(*For a full list of publications please see facing page)
1972:	Awarded the Padma Shri
1972:	Nominated to Magnum Photos (Accepted nomination in 1977)
1978-81:	Picture editor, *Sunday*
1982-92:	Picture editor, *India Today*
1990-97:	On the Jury of World Press Photo (thrice)
1992:	Awarded Photographer of the Year, USA
2005:	Retrospective at Musei Capitolini, Rome
2007:	Raghu Rai's Retrospective, Arles Photography Festival
	Raghu Rai's Retrospective, Barcelona and Madrid
2008:	Knight of Ordre des Arts et des Lettres (Knight of the Order of Arts and Letters)
2008:	Asiatica Film Mediale, Rome
2008:	Raghu Rai—A Retrospective, National Gallery of Modern Art, New Delhi
	Raghu Rai—A Retrospective, National Gallery of Modern Art, Mumbai
2010:	Raghu Rai—A Retrospective, Aicon Gallery, London
2011:	Women Changing India, Saatchi Gallery, London

Picture Index

Although the pictures are arranged chronologically for the most part, occasionally a picture will appear out of chronological sequence because of design considerations. Also, in a few cases where I cannot recall the exact date in which a picture was taken, I have given an approximate time frame.
Raghu Rai

ppii-iii Dust storm in Rajasthan, 1969
pvi Dargah in Kerala, circa 1990
p12 Baby donkey, 1965
p13 Sparrows, Chawri Bazaar, circa 1965
pp14-15 Street scene, Chawri Bazaar, circa 1966
16-17 Wheat threshing, Humayun's Tomb, 1966
p18 My father and my son, 1969
p19 Boys Jump into a village pond, 1969
p20-21 Death of Lal Bahadur Shastri, 1966
p22 Indira Gandhi in a huddle of Congressmen, 1967
p23 Indira Gandhi in her office late at night, 1968
p24 Indira in a Congress meeting, 1969
p25 Indira Gandhi at a Congress session, 1966
pp28, 29 Mother Teresa, 1970
p31 Bangladesh War, 1971
pp32-33 Bangladesh, 1971
pp34-35 Prisoner of War, 1971
p36 Instrument of Surrender, 1971
p37 General Manekshaw's moustache, 1973
p38 Gandhi and Bhutto in Shimla, 1972
p39 Indira Gandhi, 1972
pp40-41 Smiling Buddha, 1974
pp42-43 Protests, 1975
p44 Emergency, 1975
p45 Defeat, 1977
p46 Mrs Gandhi with Acharya Vinoba Bhave, 1977
p47 JP and Morarji Desai, 1978
pp48-49 Taj Mahal, 1985
pp50-51 Kalachakra initiation in Ladakh, 1976
p52 The ghats at Varanasi, 1975
p53 Varanasi, 1975

pp54-55 Diving at the Baoli, 1971
p56 Rocks near Qutab Minar, 1990
p57 Birdie girl, Humayun's Tomb, 1973
p58 The spectrum of life against a wall, circa 1975
p59 The streets of Delhi, 1976
p60 Ice hockey, 1975
p61 Flash floods in Jaipur, 1977
pp64-65 Evening prayer, Jama Masjid, 1982
pp66-67 After Durga Visarjan on the banks of the Hooghly in Kolkata, 1987
pp68-69 Morning rituals at Mulick Ghat, Kolkata, 1989
pp70-71 Relics of the past, 1992
p72 Monsoon downpour in Delhi, 1984
p73 Modern India and the people who make it, 1982
p74 Soft light and shadows in the mountains, 1982
p75 Chaiwala, Delhi–Mumbai train, 1982
p76, 77 Portraits of a painter family, 1980
p78 His Holiness the Dalai Lama, 1975
p79 His Holiness the Dalai Lama, 1989
pp80-81 Back in power, 1980
p82 Bhindranwale at the Akal Takht, 1984
p83 After Operation Blue Star, 1984
p84 End of an era, 1984
p85 Rajiv Gandhi at his mother's funeral, 1984
p86 Bhopal Gas Tragedy, 1984
p87 Burial of an unknown child, 1984
p88 Leonid Brezhnev, 1980
p89 Zia ul Haq, 1987
p90 Washing clothes, Gandhi Nagar, Delhi, 1989

p91 Wrestlers at an akhara near Paharaganj, 1988
pp92-93 Pre-monsoon clouds rise into a dust
    storm at Red Fort, 1986
pp94-95 Seagulls converging on the River
    Yamuna in Delhi, 1989
pp96-97 Pandit Ravi Shankar by the Ganga,
    1986
p98 M.S. Subbulakshmi, 1987
p99 Bhimsen Joshi, 1986
p100 Above} Hariprasad Chaurasia, 1988;
    Below} S. Balachander, 1988
101 Ustad Bismillah Khan, 1988
pp102-103 Satyajit Ray, 1989
pp106-107 Ayodhya, 1992
p108, 109 Ayodhya, 1992
p110, 111 Congress session in Tirupati, 1992
pp112-113 Mother Teresa, 1995
pp114-115 His Holiness the Dalai Lama, 1993
p116 A spiritual quiet, Mexico, 1999
p117 Paris, 1998
p118 Fall of the Soviet Union, Moscow, 1991
p119 Jerusalem, 1994
p120 Toy train to Darjeeling, 1996
p121 Churchgate Railway Station, Mumbai, 1996
p122, 123 Kargil, 1999
pp124-125 Monsoon in Mumbai, 1994
pp126-127 Mango trees near Haridwar, 1996
pp128-129 Manikarnika Ghat, 1994
pp130-131 On a beach in Mahabalipuram, 1995
pp132-133 Cow at Kandla Port, Gujarat, 1996
pp136-137 Ganesh Visarjan in Mumbai, 2002
pp138-139 Visitors at Kanyakumari, 2006
pp140-141 Wrestling akhara at Babughat, Kolkata,
    2004
p142 Men holding a rope on a construction site,
    2000

p143 The cacophony of a Kolkata street, 2004
p145 Portrait of Bal Thackeray, 2002
p146, 147 Varanasi, 2007
p148 Sadhu in Allahabad at Kumbh Mela, 2001
p149 Woman in a meditative trance, Varanasi,
    2008
pp150-151 Kumartuli in Kolkata, 2009
pp152-153 Artist's Studio in Kumartuli, Kolkata,
    2004
pp154-155 Akshardham Temple, 2005
p156 Mornings in Varanasi, 1976
p157 A young girl in her free-spirited moments,
    2006
p158 Marine Drive, Mumbai, 2008
p159 Children selling flowers at Marine Drive,
    2008
p160, 161 Up in the air, 2009
pp164-165 Family holiday in Goa, 2010
p166 River Brahmaputra, Arunachal Pradesh, 2011
p167 Maheshwar Ghat in Madhya Pradesh, 2011
pp168-169 Above} Beach in Mahabalipuram
    Below} Jantar Mantar in Jaipur, 2015
p170, 171 Backdrop series in Rajasthan, 2010
p172 Sadhus at Mahakumbh, 2013
p173 Naga sadhus, 2013
pp174-175 Leh, Ladakh, 2014
p177 Above} From the 'Trees' series, 2014
    Below} Hampi, 2012
pp178-179; 180; 181 Stone boulders in Hampi,
    Karnataka, 2012
pp182-183 View of the Lamayuru Monastery,
    Ladakh, 2000
pp184-185 Surreal landscape, Ladakh, 2014
pp186-187 The spirit of light, Ladakh, 2014
p188 The catalogue of my first exhibition, 1969
p189 In Jhang, 1987
p192 Self-portrait, 2015

Self-portrait, 2015